STALINISM

Studies in European History

General Editor: Richard Overy
Editorial Consultants: John Breuilly & Roy Porter

PUBLISHED TITLES:

FORTHCOMING

Stalinism

Second Edition

Graeme Gill

Professor of Government and Public Administration
University of Sydney

Published in Great Britain by
MACMILLAN PRESS LTD
Houndmills, Basingstoke, Hampshire RG21 6XS and London
Companies and representatives throughout the world

A catalogue record for this book is available from the British Library.

ISBN 0–333–67229–1

First edition 1990
Second edition 1998

 Published in the United States of America by
ST. MARTIN'S PRESS, INC.,
Scholarly and Reference Division,
175 Fifth Avenue, New York, N.Y. 10010

ISBN 0–312–17764–X

First edition (Humanities Press) 1990
Second edition St. Martin's Press 1998

Library of Congress Cataloging-in-Publication Data
Gill, Graeme.
Stalinism : Graeme Gill. — 2nd ed.
p.   cm.
Includes bibliographical references (p.   ) and index.
ISBN 0–312–17764–X (cloth)
1. Soviet Union—Politics and government—1936–1953.   2. Stalin,
Joseph, 1879–1953.   3. Communism—Soviet Union—History.   I. Title.
DK267.G535 1998
947.084'2—dc21   97–28331
                                                             CIP

© Graeme Gill 1990, 1998

This book is printed on paper suitable for recycling and made from fully managed and sustained forest sources.

10   9   8   7   6   5   4   3   2   1
07   06   05   04   03   02   01   00   99   98

Printed in Malaysia

Contents

Note on References

References are cited throughout in brackets according to the numbering in the general bibliography, with page references where necessary indicated by a colon after the bibliography number.

Editor's Preface

The main purpose of this Macmillan series is to make available to teacher and student alike developments in a field of history that has become increasingly specialised with the sheer volume of new research and literature now produced. These studies are designed to present the state of the debate on important themes and episodes in European history since the sixteenth century, presented in a clear and critical way by someone who is closely concerned with the debate in question.

The studies are not intended to be read as extended bibliographical essays, though each will contain a detailed guide to further reading which will lead students and the general reader quickly to key publications. Each book carries its own interpretation and conclusions, while locating the discussion firmly in the centre of the current issues as historians see them. It is intended that the series will introduce students to historical approaches which are in some cases very new and which, in the normal course of things, would take many years to filter down into the textbooks and school histories. I hope it will demonstrate some of the excitement historians, like scientists, feel as they work away in the vanguard of their subject.

The format of the series conforms closely with that of the companion volumes of studies in economic and social history which has already established a major reputation since its inception in 1968. Both series have an important contribution to make in publicising what it is that historians are doing and in making history more open and accessible. It is vital for history to communicate if it is to survive.

R. J. OVERY

Preface to Second Edition

When the first edition of this book went to press, the Soviet Union was still in existence and the question of Stalinism was one of immediate political significance in that country. The term 'Stalinism' had come to signify all that was wrong with the Soviet regime, so that the discovery and publication of information about the darker sides of Soviet history had not only a socially cathartic effect, but a politically delegitimising one as well. Analysis of Stalinism was not just a scholarly activity, but an intensely political one. With the collapse of the Soviet Union, the political imperative has become less pressing, and accordingly, the study and analysis of Stalinism within Russia has become less popular. Nevertheless the importance of understanding this phenomenon remains. The gaining of such understanding has been made somewhat easier by the increased freedom of intellectual endeavour and the opening of the archives, at least partially, in Russia. In this light it seemed appropriate to update the first edition of this volume. In doing so, I have added one new chapter and gone over the whole text making changes where this seemed appropriate. I have not felt it necessary to change the arguments in the light of new information; indeed, Western scholars of this period generally should be gratified that the revelations from the archives have tended to add details to our knowledge rather than shake many of the accepted interpretations. In any event, in addition to the new chapter and a new section of the bibliography, the text has been tinkered with and added to rather than rewritten in root and branch fashion.

Like the first edition, the aim of the book is to survey the literature dealing with Stalinism, provide a rounded analysis of what Stalinism means, and suggest a line of investigation to be pursued if we are to understand the origins of this system. The book does not provide a complete analysis of the origins of Stalinism. Nor is it a history of the Soviet Union during the Stalinist period. It is assumed that readers are basically familiar with the course of events. As a result, the book is synthetic and its arguments are skeletal rather than fully elaborated. Furthermore it is a personal view. The lines of explanation and interpretation are unlikely to meet with universal assent. I have tried to suggest through the text and the Select Bibliography (which has been restricted to English-language works but remains by no means exhaustive) where alternative views may be found.

Chronology

Feb. 1917	Fall of tsar; establishment of Provisional Government
Oct. 1917	Bolshevik seizure of power
Jan. 1918	Dissolution of Constituent Assembly
Mar. 1918	Brest-Litovsk Treaty ends war with Germany; coalition government with SRs ends; government moves from Petrograd to Moscow
June 1918	Large-scale nationalisation of industry; civil war begins; War Communism
Mar. 1919	VIII Congress of Communist Party and defeat of Military Opposition; formal establishment of Politburo, Orgburo and Secretariat
Oct.–Dec. 1919	Major defeats of White armies in south; withdrawal of foreign troops from Russia
Apr.–Oct. 1920	War with Poland
Nov.–Dec. 1920	End of civil war
Mar. 1921	X Congress of Communist Party; NEP introduced; defeat of Democratic Centralists and Workers' Opposition; 'On Party Unity' resolution; suppression of Kronstadt rebellion
Apr. 1922	Stalin becomes General Secretary of CC
May 1922	Lenin's first serious illness
Mar. 1923	Lenin's second stroke removes him from political life; triumvirate of Stalin, Zinoviev and Kamenev formed to attack Trotsky
Jan. 1924	Lenin dies; struggle with Trotsky intensifies
1925	Defeat of Trotsky; triumvirate splits
Dec. 1925	XIV Congress of Communist Party; Stalin defeats Zinoviev and Kamenev; they join Trotsky in United Opposition
May 1927	Diplomatic relations broken with Britain; heightens war scare

Dec. 1927	XV Congress of Communist Party calls for a speed up in industrialisation and agricultural collectivisation; United Opposition defeated; Trotsky expelled from party and many of his supporters exiled
Jan.–Feb. 1928	Stalin uses coercion to overcome grain procurement crisis; Stalin's rift with Bukharin widens
Mar. 1928	Shakhty affair
Feb. 1929	Trotsky deported from USSR
Apr. 1929	Defeat of Bukharin
Nov. 1929	Bukharin removed from Politburo; full-scale collectivisation announced
Dec. 1929	Cult of Stalin begins
1930–4	'Revolution from above' – forced-pace industrialisation and collectivisation, rapid social mobility, culture tied to production
Mar. 1930	Stalin's 'Dizzy with success' article calls a temporary halt in collectivisation
late 1930	Syrtsov–Lominadze group
Nov.–Dec. 1930	Trial of Industrial Party 'saboteurs'
Mar. 1931	Trial of the Menshevik 'saboteurs'
June–Dec. 1932	Riutin Platform and Eismont–Tolmachev–Smirnov group
Dec. 1932	First Five Year Plan declared completed in 4.5 years
end 1932–3	Famine in southern grain-producing areas
Apr. 1933	Trial of Metro-Vickers engineers as 'wreckers and saboteurs'
1933–4	Official party purge
Jan.–Feb. 1934	XVII Congress of Communist Party; some opposition to Stalin
Apr. 1934	Zhdanov introduces 'socialist realism'
Dec. 1934	Assassination of Kirov
1935	Campaign for verification of party documents
1936	Campaign for exchange of party cards
Aug. 1936	Trial of 'Trotskyite-Zinovievite Terrorist Centre' (Zinoviev, Kamenev *et al.*)
Sept. 1936	Ezhov appointed head of NKVD; intensifies terror
Dec. 1936	Adoption of 'Stalin Constitution'
1937	Ezhovshchina; purges and terror climax
Jan. 1937	Trial of 'Anti-Soviet Trotskyite Centre' (Piatakov, Radek *et al.*)

June. 1937	Leading military figures purged
Mar. 1938	Trial of 'Anti-Soviet Bloc of Rights and Trotskyites'(Bukharin, Rykov *et al.*)
Dec. 1938	Ezhov replaced by Beria as NKVD head
Aug. 1939	Nazi-Soviet Pact signed
Nov. 1939– Mar. 1940	War with Finland
1940	Incorporation of Baltic republics and part of Romania
May 1941	Stalin becomes Chairman of the Council of People's Commissars
June 1941	German attack on USSR; establishment of State Defence Committee
1943–4	Deportation of small national groups accused of collaboration with Germans
May 1945	End of war in Europe
Sept. 1945	End of war with Japan
1945–8	Consolidation of Soviet control in Eastern Europe
Aug. 1946	Decision 'On the Journals *Zvezda* and *Leningrad*' reimposing cultural conformity
Feb. 1947	Only post-war CC plenum meets
Feb. 1949– Oct. 1950	Leningrad Affair
1951–2	Mingrelian case
Oct. 1952	XIX Congress of Communist Party
1952–3	Doctors' plot
Mar. 1953	Death of Stalin

1 Historical Roots of Stalinism?

One of the most important questions that has confronted both those interested in Soviet history and politics and those seeking to bring about fundamental socialist change has been the origins of Stalinism. This issue has been important because it raises the question of the fate of the Russian revolution and in particular why a revolution launched in the name of such laudable principles could result in the type of dictatorial political system which emerged at the end of the 1930s. For many, it also raised questions about the ultimate viability of Marxist-inspired social engineering. A satisfactory answer to this question of Stalinist origins was therefore fundamental both for scholars wishing to understand the course of Soviet development and for political actors seeking to reaffirm the validity of their ideological beliefs. It was also an important issue for many who have mined the riches available in the newly opened Soviet archives, even if they have been unable to uncover material which would lead to a major revision of our established interpretations.

A common response to this need has been to seek the 'roots' or 'seeds' of Stalinism in the pre-Stalinist period of development. Such a course of action has much to recommend it, but with one, major, qualification. Every period of history is clearly related to that which went before, and therefore has its 'roots' in that earlier time. In this sense scholars are justified in searching for elements in the pre-Stalinist period which contributed to the moulding or emergence of Stalinism. However, there has been a tendency on the part of many scholars to transform the linkages that exist between periods into firm causative, even deterministic, relations. Scholars must recognise that each period has within it the 'roots' of a variety of different courses of development, and that the discovery of the roots of a particular line of subsequent development alone does not explain why that particular line of development occurred. What must be explained is why this particular potential line of development succeeded while the rest failed. Such an explanation cannot rely on some mystical inner dynamic which is believed to inhere in the discovered roots, but must take full account of all the circumstances of the time, including the views and actions of the political actors. Therefore while we can find elements in the pre-Stalinist period that contributed to the emergence and development of Stalinism, the relationship between these elements and Stalinism is not a deterministic one. This question will be discussed further in Chapter 4.

[i] Russian backwardness

In the search for Stalinist roots in the pre-Stalinist period, some scholars have devoted attention to the nature of Russian political culture [e.g. 213; 257: *ch.1*]. While the precise emphasis in various of these explanations differs, their essence is the same: traditional Russian society was one in which the mass of the population was politically uninvolved and the state dominated society. As a result, the course of Russian development was overwhelmingly driven by state initiative, and this tended of necessity to involve significant force. Ivan the Terrible and Peter the Great were the two best exemplars of this, with Stalin simply being a Soviet version of the traditional Russian moderniser [198]. This argument gained some prominence in discussions of Stalinism in the Soviet press in the late-1980s; Vasilii Seliunin, for example, argued that Stalinism was a continuation of the tradition of state compulsion and therefore of bureaucratic dominance which, rather than market forces, had generated progress in Russia [213; 240]. This sort of approach, focusing on the strength of the state and weakness of society, also underpins another line of interpretation evident in late Soviet discussions of Stalinism and reflected in the work of Alexander Tsipko. He argues [240] that the 'sources' of Stalinism lay in the anti-bourgeois messianism of the Russian intelligentsia which, cut off from playing any meaningful role in Russian society, had little sense of practicality within which to root their theorising. This sort of approach of the radical intelligentsia, argues Tsipko, was carried forward and reinforced by the nature of Marxism.

Such culturally based arguments are difficult to sustain as explanations of the causes of Stalinism. It is easy to point to parallels between Peter the Great and Stalin and to the impracticality of much of the Russian intelligentsia. However it is less easy to identify causative connections. Society and the cultural norms which are embedded in it are neither consistent in the images of authority they project nor unchanging over time; Soviet society in 1929 was very different from that of Peter the Great in 1700 or Chernyshevsky in 1860. This does not mean that cultural aspects are not important in explaining political phenomena, only that similarities should not be confused with causal links.

Another aspect of Russian society to which significant attention has been devoted is the backwardness of Russia and its implications in the dozen years following the revolution in October 1917. The man who has done most to shape our perception of Stalin, Leon Trotsky, had this backwardness at the heart of his analysis [98; 184; 185; 186], and it has been reflected too in the works of many of those who have followed and revised him in later years [2; 31; 47; 54; 125]. For many scholars not persuaded by the Marxist mode of analysis, Russian backwardness has also been important as an explanatory factor [102; 144].

At the heart of the focus on backwardness are the low levels of economic and social development in Russia at the time of the revolution. When the Bolsheviks came to power they inherited an economy which had been devastated by three years of war; the strains imposed upon rural and urban sectors of the economy had been immense. Moreover its basic structure was essentially bifurcated. The vast bulk of the population lived in the countryside and worked on the small peasant farms that spread across the vast Russian landscape. Agricultural techniques throughout much of the countryside remained primitive, and the structure of peasant farming meant that there was very little flexibility or margin for error on the part of peasant producers; poor harvests meant considerable hardship. In the cities a new industrial infrastructure had been developing, principally as a result of the spurt in industrial growth towards the end of the last century. Factories and mills had sprung up and the working-class suburbs had been filled by the raw recruits flowing into the cities to escape the penury many would otherwise have faced in the villages. The pre-war economy had, therefore, a small, modern, developed industrial sector beside a largely backward and unwieldy agricultural sector.

The war and the revolution itself placed immense strains upon the economy. The mechanism of exchange between town and countryside collapsed, industrial production declined catastrophically, and the working class began to contract as workers headed back to their villages of origin rather than face the likelihood of unemployment and hunger in the cities. These effects were exacerbated by the policy of War Communism implemented by the Bolsheviks from the middle of 1918. This was a policy characterised by the nationalisation of industry, a ban on private trade, a rationing system for food and consumer goods, the elimination of money and the forced delivery of grain to the state. By the time this policy was reversed in March 1921, both the urban and rural economies had effectively collapsed; industrial output was approximately 31 per cent and agricultural output 60 per cent of what it had been in 1913 [139: 68].

The collapse of the national economy had important implications for the Bolsheviks. The Marxism to which they adhered had led them to believe that socialist revolution would occur first in the advanced capitalist countries, where there was a high level of industrial development. While Russia had never been that, Lenin had developed Marxist theory in such a way that it effectively legitimised socialist revolution in Russia [83]. He declared that such a revolution could break out in the weakest link of the capitalist chain, an event which would stimulate revolutions in the more highly developed states under capitalism. If such revolutions had occurred, and the strength of the world proletariat had been thrown into the scales to outweigh the predominance of the Russian peasantry over the native proletariat, not only would the unfavourable balance of class forces in Russia have been rectified, but the sense of isolation in a hostile domestic environment may not have taken hold among the Bolsheviks. But such revolutions did not occur; the Bolsheviks remained the only successful socialist revolutionaries in the world, but they had been successful in a society which seemed to lack the theoretical prerequisites for imminent socialist development. This message was made plain to the Bolsheviks by the economic collapse and corresponding erosion of their social base; between mid-1917 and late 1920, the number of factory workers in Russia declined by some 70 per cent. As the proletariat disintegrated, with large numbers of workers returning to the villages, the class upon which the party sought to base itself shrank. The sense of increasing isolation and insecurity within Bolshevik ranks mounted.

In practical terms, the party's answer to economic collapse was to introduce the New Economic Policy (NEP). This policy restored

4

private ownership and market relations in agriculture and all but the 'commanding heights' in industry; private enterprise became once again the main force of economic development. The economy was set on the course of recovery. By 1926–7 production was back to pre-war levels. But this economic regeneration also had significant negative implications in the eyes of many Bolsheviks, particularly among the leaders. The aim of the revolution had been the attainment of socialism and the elimination of capitalism from Russia. However NEP relied upon a strengthening of capitalist elements in the economy, particularly the countryside. Although Lenin had argued in the twilight of his life that through the expansion of cooperation, NEP could lead to socialism [104], many in the party saw in NEP the strengthening of control of the *kulaks*, the rich peasants, in the countryside. Party policy thus seemed, to many, to be leading to the consolidation of precisely that element against whom the revolution had been directed, the bourgeoisie.

This question was also complicated by the perceived need for fostering industrial development and the recognition by all sections of the party by 1927 that the tempo of industrialisation had to be increased substantially. The speed up in industrialisation was deemed necessary principally for security reasons. Three types of concern were evident. The first was that the continued operation of NEP and the associated strengthening of capitalism was leading to some demoralisation within party ranks and this could only be overcome by hastening the move to socialism through increased industrialisation. The sense of excitement and commitment evoked by the belief that they were engaged in building a brave new world of socialism was difficult to sustain in the face of policies promoting the strengthening of capitalist elements in the countryside. Industrialisation was seen as the key to reigniting enthusiasm for the socialist project.

The second concern related to the domestic environment and the fear of the effects of the petty bourgeois peasant context within which the party existed. It was felt that what was required was a strengthening of the position of the proletariat, something that could be achieved only through industrial expansion. If the proletariat could thus be strengthened, the danger of the degeneration of the regime as a result of swamping by the peasants would disappear, and the rule of the proletariat would be consolidated. While fears about the degeneration of the party's proletarian essence as a result of petty bourgeois peasant infection were ideological in nature, these also had a practical aspect: it was the hostile petty bourgeois peasants who controlled the flow of grain to the cities, and therefore potentially could hold the regime to ransom. Proletarian rule therefore appeared less secure than they would have liked. The proletariat's hold on power was symbolised by the parlous situation of the party in the countryside [57; 73]; in 1928 there were only 20,660 rural party cells to cover 546,747 population centres in the countryside, and only 0.7 per cent of peasant households included a party member.

The third concern was international in nature. The opposition of the most powerful states to the Bolshevik regime had been evident from the time of the revolution. Western states were critical of the Bolsheviks' withdrawal from the war, repudiation of tsarist debts and nationalisation of foreign enterprises, and were fearful of the potential effects of Bolshevik support for socialist revolution in the West. Initially a number of them sought to overthrow the new rulers of Russia through military intervention in the civil war. When this failed, economic and trade boycotts were mounted and covert action was conducted against the Bolshevik regime. Despite the establishment of formal diplomatic relations between the Soviet Union and a number of these states during the 1920s, only with Germany did any closeness develop. Relations were always correct rather than warm, and the basis upon which they rested was always shaky. Neither side trusted the other. The Bolsheviks feared that the capitalist powers were simply awaiting an opportunity to step in and strangle the new regime, an impression that the war scare of 1927 both reflected and fuelled [63; 134]. The only protection against this could be the development of Soviet industrial and military might, and the sooner the better.

The sense of insecurity that pervaded the party was genuine. Worried that the party would degenerate as a result of its swamping by petty bourgeois peasants and convinced that there was little likelihood of any assistance coming from abroad (particularly following the failure of the Chinese revolution in 1927), this insecurity had important implications for the subsequent emergence of Stalinism. The practical means of seeking to overcome this problem, agricultural collectivisation and forced-pace industrialisation, were significant progenitors of Stalinism. But important too was the general lesson to be drawn from this environment. If both the domestic and the international context were hostile and dangerous, they could not be relied on if party aims were to be realised. Consequently, if socialism

6

was to be achieved, a leading part would have to be played by the party. This body thus appeared in the minds of many of its members as the main instrument for the achievement of social engineering, a belief that facilitated the revolution from above. It is also at the heart of one interpretation which gained some currency in the Soviet Union at the end of the 1980s, viz., the combination of backwardness, utopian socialism and the statisation of the means of production were essential factors in the origins of Stalinism [213]. It was also consistent with some of the lessons to be drawn from the written legacy of the party's founder, V. I. Lenin.

[ii] Leninism

The Leninist legacy has featured large in Western studies of Stalinism and its emergence [38: *403*; 99; 111; 166; 167; 175; 195: *198*]. Many have sought to find in Leninism the origins of Stalinism, pointing to the Leninist scheme of party organisation, the insistence on correct views, the hegemonic role attributed to intellectuals, the ruthlessness, and the emphasis upon discipline as being key impulses coming through Lenin's writings and actions which stimulated the development of Stalinism. But once again this argument needs to be treated carefully before it is accepted. In its deterministic forms, the so-called 'continuity thesis' is easily rejected [27]. It relies upon a selective quotation from the corpus of Lenin's writings and a partial interpretation of both the Leninist and Stalinist periods. In its worst forms it can be mechanistic and deny any scope for individual activity on the part of political actors. Indeed, it is this failure to take into account the autonomy of political actors which is its greatest failing.

The Leninist heritage was rich and varied fare for those who followed Lenin [27; 72]. There were certainly elements in both Leninism and Bolshevism which were consistent with the type of system which emerged at the end of the 1930s. The authoritarian strand of the Bolshevik tradition, to which the writings and actions of Lenin and other Bolshevik leaders at times contributed, provided a programme emphasising central control, discipline and ideological orthodoxy. This strand was consistent with but did not generate the highly centralised political system of Stalinism. The more democratic strand of Bolshevism emphasised rank-and-file sovereignty, widespread discussion, and the legitimacy of intra-party opposition, all of which were reflected in the writings and activities at different times of Lenin and other Bolshevik leaders. These were completely antithetical to Stalinism. In this sense, the pre-revolutionary tradition, including its Leninist stream, offered a variety of potential courses of development for the party. None was foreordained, and the victory of a set of arrangements which more closely matched the authoritarian than the democratic strand was the result of political choices by the relevant political actors. It was not the result of some mythical inner essence of either Bolshevism or Leninism, even though those supporting the development of a more authoritarian structure may have sought guidance from their understanding of Lenin's thought and certainly sought to justify their actions by reference to Lenin.

The political development of the Soviet regime was the result not of a carefully designed blueprint laid down in advance, but of a series of almost *ad hoc* decisions designed to structure political life in the new state. Despite the existence of a coalition government with the Left SRs between November 1917 and March 1918, there is no evidence that Lenin (as opposed to some of his colleagues) ever seriously considered the creation of anything but a one-party state as desirable. Indeed, it was during this initial period of Bolshevik rule that major decisions were taken which closed off alternative potential avenues of political activity: the closure of the Constituent Assembly, the suppression of other political parties, the elimination of press freedom and the establishment of party control over the soviets all occurred in the early years of Bolshevik rule [167]. These moves effectively limited popular access to the political sphere to the channels controlled by the party (chiefly the soviets) or the party itself, and by 1920 had rendered any notion of unfettered competitive politics impossible.

This limitation of legitimate political activity to the party and to party-controlled arenas did help to lay the groundwork which made a Stalinist regime possible. It eliminated the possibility of legitimate opposition outside the party and, perhaps more importantly, gave those sections of society which opposed the Bolsheviks no vehicle through which to exercise that opposition. Implicitly the principle of societal unanimity was established, thereby eliminating the scope for a vigorous public life. However, the limitation of legitimate political activity to the party and party-dominated arenas during Lenin's lifetime had no *necessary* or *inevitable* consequences for the future structuring of political life in the party; they could have been overturned had the political will been present. However in the absence of such political will, they continued to help structure the contours of Soviet political life.

[iii] The personal factor

Explanations for the rise of Stalinism often give significant attention to the personal role of Stalin [40; 47; 87; 166; 194; 259]. One element of this focus on Stalin's personal role that is often found in analyses of this problem is Stalin's personality. For some, what is important is Stalin's abilities [230]. Rather than the mediocrity mocked by Trotsky, he was said to be cool and calculating, a first rate political tactician and behind the scenes fighter, someone who could plot and intrigue and thereby outwit his opponents. His capacity for hard work, and especially his ability to master the routine and perceived drudgery of day-to-day administrative work in the party bureaucracy have also been seen as important qualities. For others [e.g. 190], what is important is his personal qualities. He was said by some to be cruel, vindictive, easy to take offence and liable to bear grudges (although family portraits do not give such a picture [3; 4]). Some saw him as suffering from an inferiority complex, perhaps because of physical afflictions (webbed toes, withered arm, pock-marked face and short stature are all pointed to in this regard) or because he clearly lacked the public profile and stature of many of his fellow Bolsheviks; for Robert Tucker, he was driven to be a new Lenin, with the 'revolution from above' the analogue of 'Great October'. In any event, all of these views have Stalin trying to compensate for something by gaining ultimate power. Clearly Stalin's personal features and idiosyncrasies were instrumental in his drive for power and the later shaping of Stalinism, but we cannot build the nature of the whole system on the edifice of individual personality. Too many other people and factors were important.

Of central importance in discussions of the personal role of Stalin is the power he was able to exercise over personnel distribution within the party, a power which enabled him to appoint his supporters to positions of responsibility throughout the party structure. Central to this explanation is Stalin's institutional position in the central party apparatus. Following his appointment as General Secretary in

April 1922, Stalin was the only member of the Bolshevik elite who was simultaneously a full member of the Central Committee's three executive organs, the Politburo, Orgburo and Secretariat. All had been formally established in 1919. The Politburo was the major arena of political decision-making, while the other two organs were concerned with internal party administration, including personnel questions. Control over the Orgburo and Secretariat, which Stalin was able to achieve, gave control over personnel appointment, and thereby the capacity to stack party bodies with those prepared to carry out his will.

This explanation has some validity, but needs to be attended by significant qualifications. Stalin's position as General Secretary and his ability to insert his supporters into the Central Committee Secretariat enabled him to dominate questions of personnel selection from the early-mid-1920s. However, the party machine throughout this period was insufficiently developed to be able to ensure that the centre could exercise continuing control over events at lower party levels. While the centre could certainly intervene and remove individual party leaders at subnational levels, it could not exercise continuing close monitoring of what local leaders were doing. Channels of communication between centre and localities were underdeveloped, while the central party apparatus was not an efficient, smoothly-operating machine. Local party leaders were able to rule almost as they liked; corruption and abuse of power at these levels was common, with local leaders often living a life of comparative luxury and self-indulgence. The organisational ties between centre and lower officials were therefore looser than has often been assumed and certainly were not sufficiently strong to enable us to talk of a solid, highly organised and disciplined Stalin machine [73; 75; 76].

Part of the standard explanation has been that these lower level officials, having been appointed by Stalin and owing their positions to him, were his obedient supporters throughout the factional struggles of the 1920s. However, the weakness of the institutional mechanisms for maintaining tight central control meant that these lower-level leaders, in practice, had greater autonomy than the standard explanation has assumed. This means that instead of being able to rely upon the automatic support of these lower level functionaries, Stalin had to work at gaining that support. In effect, he had to be able to construct alliances with the lower-level leaders, something he was able to do with considerable success until 1927–8 when the development

10

of distrust between General Secretary and lower-level leaders began to gather pace [73; 76].

The background to the establishment of this alliance was the succession of conflicts which wracked the party between 1917 and 1929. Initially, the conflict pitted a nominally united leadership against dissident groups with their roots at lower levels of the party. The Left Communists in 1918, Military Opposition in 1919, and Democratic Centralists and Workers' Opposition in 1920–1 hoisted their battle standards against the prevailing line of party policy, only to be defeated on the floor of successive party congresses. It was at the X Congress of the party in March 1921, against a background of widespread peasant unrest, discontent in the cities and the rising of the Kronstadt sailors, that the Democratic Centralists and Workers' Opposition were finally defeated and that the famous resolution 'On Party Unity' was introduced. This has been seen by many as constituting a turning point in party history and as being an important step that set the party ineluctably on the course to Stalinism [167]. Certainly before this resolution the prevailing sentiment was that opposition was a legitimate right within the party, providing of course that such activity was restricted strictly to party ranks. 'On Party Unity' effectively changed the official position by outlawing all fractions, defined as groups 'based on some platform or other' and making those who engaged in fractional activity subject to expulsion from the party. In effect, it thereby rendered opposition formally illegal in the party. But we must be careful not to attribute too much to this resolution. The history of the party was littered with resolutions which lost their force virtually as soon as they had been adopted. Furthermore the same congress as that which had adopted the 'On Party Unity' resolution had encouraged free discussion within the party, something which did not sit well with the restrictions imposed by this resolution. This means that 'On Party Unity' served to reduce opposition and stifle debate only in so far as it was used in these fashions by political leaders. The resolution was important not because of anything that flowed automatically from it, but because it was useful as a weapon to be wielded against dissent by the leadership group around Stalin.

In the years following Lenin's illness and subsequent death, the unity of the leadership was split by a succession of conflicts between the leading figures of the regime. The playing out of these conflicts all resulted in the victory of the group surrounding Stalin

11

over successive opposition groups. Following Lenin's death in January 1924, Stalin joined with Zinoviev and Kamenev to overcome Trotsky and his supporters in a conflict characterised by debate about the future of the revolution which saw the emergence of the doctrine 'socialism in one country' (see below). With Trotsky defeated by early 1925, Stalin's alliance with Zinoviev and Kamenev disinte-grated, and the former allies now came into conflict. In Stalin's struggle against this so-called 'Left Opposition', the meaning of 'so-cialism in one country' and the attitude the party should adopt to the peasantry were major elements in the debate. The Left was van-quished by the beginning of 1926. Stalin had then to confront the so-called 'United Opposition', led by Trotsky, Zinoviev and Kamenev. Supported by Bukharin among others, Stalin was able to defeat his foes by the end of 1927. Now Stalin split with his erstwhile sup-porters, chiefly Bukharin, Rykov and Tomsky, over the question of the fate of NEP. This group, the 'Right Opposition', was defeated by April 1929. In each of these conflicts, with the possible excep-tion of that against the Right, most lower-level party leaders sup-ported Stalin. Why were Stalin and his successive groups of elite colleagues able to defeat these different opposition groups, particu-larly when these groups seemed to boast party leaders of far higher standing than Stalin?

Stalin's use of the organisational weapon was important. Although the limitations of the party's organisational machinery prevented the maintenance of close, continuing control over lower-level party leaders, Stalin could wield his personnel powers in such a way as to break up the organisational power bases held by his opponents. Perhaps the most famous cases of this were the destruction of Zinoviev's base in Leningrad in 1926, when Stalin was able to overturn what appeared to be Zinoviev's firmly based local dictatorship with only a few weeks work by his supporters, and his destruction of Uglanov's Rightist organisation in Moscow at the end of the 1920s [236]. These were merely illustrative of a power which extended throughout the party machine. But equally important was his ability to win over the support of party leaders at all levels. Stalin was able to do this in part because of the policy positions he espoused and in part be-cause of the authority he was able to project. In terms of policy, Stalin espoused positions which lower-level leaders found conge-nial. His advocacy of the doctrine of 'socialism in one country' promised the chance of the successful achievement of socialism on the basis of their own efforts rather than having to be rescued by international revolution, which seemed to be the implication of Trotsky's more internationalist outlook. This was a powerful argument in the ideological context of Russian backwardness. On economic policy throughout the middle of the decade, he was associated with moderate, centrist policies that seemed to promise continued advance, but then towards the end of the 1920s when the perception that NEP was running into the sand began to take hold, he seemed to offer a way out. Furthermore, each of the opposition groups criticised the lack of democracy in the party, thereby calling into question the means whereby party leaders gained and held their offices. This sort of attack could not help but drive lower-level party leaders away from the opposition and towards the person who stood at the head of the party apparatus of which they were part, Stalin. Successive opposition groups could also be discredited by the way in which they were presented as challenging the status quo within the party, thereby making them vulnerable to the charge that they were violating the fundamental Leninist principle of party unity.

But Stalin was also able to consolidate his support by manipulating the symbolic universe of the regime [74]. He was able in a much more skilful fashion than his competitors to attach himself to the growing cult of Lenin and the myth of October which gave a sense of legitimacy to the regime. By doing so, he made it difficult to attack him without appearing to attack either Lenin or October. This symbolic manipulation was particularly important because of the large number of party members who were new to the party. The party increased from 24,000 in 1917 to 1,677,910 in 1930. The numbers entering the party were actually much higher than these figures suggest because there was a significant wastage as a result of purges like those of 1921 and 1929–30, regular housekeeping operations throughout the 1920s, the voluntary departure of party members and natural causes [154]. Most of the new members had no ideological knowledge and the simplistic symbols projected by Stalin therefore appealed to them and to their perceived need to demonstrate their good party credentials by mastering the ideology. Stalin's book *Foundations of Leninism*, published in 1924, was particularly important in this regard. So too was the process of historical revision which was being fostered by Stalin and his supporters at this time. It is clear, therefore, that Stalin was better able than his opponents to establish a sense of his authority within party ranks.

Stalin was aided in this by the fact that his political skills and acumen far outweighed those of his rivals; he was a better political tactician, less inclined to the grand histrionic gesture, more adept at the manipulative manoeuvrings that were an essential part of party politics, and better able to pitch his appeal at a level which was attractive to wide sections of the party. Beside his political skills, his opponents seemed like novices, making elementary mistakes which ultimately proved fatal. The failure of Stalin's opponents to use Lenin's 'testament' in which he called for Stalin's removal at the XIII Congress in 1924 was perhaps the best opportunity they had to strike a decisive blow against the General Secretary. Trotsky refused either to attempt to organise in his own defence or to tailor his message to garner rank-and-file support, instead relying upon his revolutionary stature to carry him to victory. The Zinoviev–Kamenev–Trotsky alliance lacked credibility from the outset given the recent vitriolic exchanges between the leaders when they had been opposed to one another. Like Trotsky, Bukharin made little attempt to build up a power base from which he could defend himself against Stalin. Stalin's opponents were thus much less adept at political infighting than the General Secretary, and were not as quick to see that power stemmed from organisational position in the apparatus, and they paid dearly for this.

What is clear is that by the end of the 1920s Stalin had been able to establish himself as the leading person in the party leadership. But he had been able to do this not because he had a highly disciplined, organised political machine to do his bidding, but because he was able to play the rules of the political game and to generate political support far more ably than his opponents. Furthermore the leadership of which he was a part did not consist solely of his creatures. They all had party careers which pre-dated their association with Stalin and they were all party leaders in their own right. They therefore all retained a degree of autonomy from the General Secretary. Nevertheless the leadership was clearly different in nature from that which had been at the apex of the party under Lenin: the range of intellectual ability and interests of the Stalinist leadership was lower and their importance in the history of the party was less than those they defeated during the 1920s. The second echelon of party leaders had moved into positions of power.

What does this mean for the roots of Stalinism? The defeat of the successive opposition groups, plus the tenets of 'On Party Unity', did not mean that opposition would not occur in the future, but it did alter the methods whereby such opposition could operate. In doing so, it rendered all opposition illegal, and therefore provided the leadership with a major weapon with which to defeat any opposition which happened subsequently to emerge. But this, like the elimination of public channels of politics, was not something that was cast in stone. Nothing automatically flowed from it independently of action taken by the leading political actors. The Stalinist political system as it existed from the end of the 1930s would not have emerged from the situation that existed at the time of the defeat of the Right Opposition without major decisions having been made by leading political actors. Neither the continuity thesis nor the simple fact of Russian backwardness can explain the genesis of the Stalinist system. Nor can a focus purely on the person of Stalin.

2 Stalinism Established

Anyone surveying the Soviet scene in 1927 would have seen a so-ciety in which there was little direct evidence of the Stalinism that was to come. The principal axis of the economy was still the opera-tion of market principles with private enterprise, particularly in ag-riculture, operating alongside those 'commanding heights' which were under direct state control. Cultural life remained vigorous, and al-though there were clear restrictions on what could be published and performed, the boundaries of this were much wider and more re-laxed than they had been either during War Communism or than they were to become. Notions of class struggle and of the construction of socialism were not overpowering themes, while the emphasis was upon reconciliation with all social forces, including ideologically suspect groups like the intelligentsia and the so-called 'bourgeois specialists'. The more relaxed cultural sphere reflected this sense of compromise, and resulted in a ferment of ideas, of cultural variety and pluralism. Socially, NEP witnessed the re-emergence of stratifi-cation along traditional lines. In the countryside, some farmers were able to build up their economic bases and to establish a position of economic leadership in the villages. These were later to be labelled *kulaks*. In the towns too, differentiated incomes led to stratification, with owners of capital once again being higher on the ladder than those they employed to work in their factories and workshops. Cer-tainly some avenues for upward mobility had opened up for the workers and peasants under the new regime, particularly through the revitalisation of industry, the expansion of the bureaucracy and the growth of the party, but these remained restricted. In political terms, while the avenues for public politics had been closed, the mould of elite politics within the party had not yet been set. Open opposition had been eliminated, and politics remained oligarchical in form. The continued operation of a sense of collectivism, albeit with Stalin emerging as the most important figure, contrasts sharply

16

with the personal dictatorship that was to characterise Stalinism.

In all of these areas – economic, cultural, social and political – Stalinism was to provide a sharp contrast with the situation at the end of the NEP. There was no direct line of self-generated development between late NEP and Stalinism; the four faces of Stalinism, the economic, cultural, social and political, all diverged sharply from their NEPist counterparts. Their introduction required the breaking of the mould that was setting under NEP. In the case of the economic, cultural and social faces, this was achieved through the 'revolution from above' at the end of the 1920s–early 1930s. For the political, it was to come about through the terror.

[i] 'Revolution from above'

The beginning of the 'revolution from above' came in January 1928 when Stalin sought to extract grain from the peasants of Siberia [41; 106]. In response to the grain procurement crisis that became apparent at the end of 1927, Stalin resorted to what were acknowledged to be 'extraordinary measures' in an attempt to increase the flow of grain into the collection points. The use of extraordinary measures had been accepted by the Politburo, but Stalin clearly exceeded his authority and that body's wishes through the extensive use of force, coercion and grain seizure which he fostered. The use of these methods was restricted both in terms of regions and time in 1928, but they were resorted to once again in 1929. With the Right Opposition defeated by April 1929, this means of grain collection was escalated into the full-blown attack on the peasantry which agricultural collectivisation constituted.

At the XV Congress of the party in December 1927, the First Five Year Plan had been introduced. This had called for increased emphasis upon the development of heavy industry and for the fostering of agricultural producers' cooperatives, although it was acknowledged that private production would remain the basis of agriculture for some time to come. Moreover, coercion was not to be used to force the bulk of the middle peasants into the new cooperatives. However, these moderate goals were soon overthrown. In December 1929 it was decided that the plan would be achieved in four years, not five, and during this period a continual process of revising plan targets upward was set in motion. Collectivisation was to be completed in the major grain-producing areas by spring of 1932, and the *kulaks* were to be liquidated as a class, thereby explicitly associating economic restructuring with social engineering; the establishment of collective agriculture was to involve the destruction of a particular class of peasants. Plan targets ceased to reflect rational calculations about economic possibilities, and came to represent purely the preferences of the political leadership.

The reasons for this dramatic change in the party's economic policy have been reviewed extensively in Western scholarship [41; 106; 136; 141]. Despite the fact that collectivised agriculture was a net drain on the state's resources immediately following collectivisation, with more resources having to be committed to agriculture than were forthcoming from agriculture for investment elsewhere in the economy, it was hoped that collectivisation would be the means of ensuring that the state was able to get the financial and labour resources from agriculture which it needed to pursue its industrialisation plans [136]. Of course, resources could have been siphoned from agriculture through the continued operation of the market system of NEP, as the Right had argued [28]. But such a course of action would not have met the objection that the regime was being held to ransom by the peasant producers, who, it was believed, used their control over grain supply to wring concessions from the authorities; the procurement crisis at the end of 1927 was seen as evidence of this charge. Neither would it have met the perceived need for speedy industrial development which was present at this time (see Chapter 1). Furthermore a course of action which involved the elimination of the private entrepreneur and the smashing of market principles gained sustenance from the understanding of Marxist ideology possessed by many long-term party members. Although there was clearly a counter theme in the ideology, reflected in the broad ideological justifications given for NEP, the revival of the sense of struggling directly to build socialism and the consequent sense of meaning that this gave to many party members, ensured that this more 'heroic' strand of the ideology prevailed over the routine, status quo orientation of the pro-NEP strand; the militant enthusiasm of the War Communism period returned [28]. None of these imperatives were perceived to be consistent with the continuation of NEP supported by the Right.

The effect of the 'revolution from above' was momentous and its implementation searing for the society. The course of agricultural collectivisation was chaotic and characterised by significant levels of coercion. No adequate preparation had been carried out, instructions from the centre gave little concrete direction to local political activists about how to achieve the centre's goals, and all the time there was a prevailing sense of searching for and rooting out enemies which encouraged many to err on the side of harshness when dealing with recalcitrant peasants [106]. There was widespread peasant opposition, reflected both in armed attempts to prevent the implementation of central policy, and in the destruction of crops and livestock. Although opposition was particularly marked among those who were labelled *kulaks* and who were therefore subject to the policy of dekulakisation (which effectively meant shooting or deportation to north Russia or Siberia), such sentiments were present among wide sections of the peasantry. Millions of peasants died during the course of collectivisation and dekulakisation, and particularly during the famine of 1932–3 which struck at the Ukraine and the grain-producing areas of the North Caucasus [34]. In the short term, collectivisation constituted a significant setback to the economy, with much of the agricultural infrastructure destroyed; beside the farms that were disrupted and the equipment that was destroyed, the Soviet livestock herd decreased alarmingly between 1928 and 1933, the number of cattle, pigs, and sheep and goats fell, respectively, by 45.5, 53.5 and 65.8 per cent [140: *44*]. The principal longer term effect of collectivisation was that it firmly placed the peasantry under state control and thereby guaranteed continuing state access to the grain resources of the country. Large-scale private agriculture was eliminated, although the right to farm small private plots was introduced in 1935.

In the industrial sector too, rapid transformation was evident during the First Five Year Plan. The primary emphasis was placed upon the development of heavy industry, with the result that the established industrial centres in the country were refurbished and expanded and completely new industrial centres were built from the ground up. Inevitably such industrial development was patchy. The speed demanded often created waste and shoddiness, but at the same time the industrial infrastructure which lifted the USSR into the status of a superpower was created.

During the First Five Year Plan (1928–32) a new form of economic system was created. Market principles were replaced by central direction as the key guiding force of the economy. Henceforth

19

the succession of five year plans were to be the principal levers of economic life. All decisions about economic matters were to be shifted to the planning authorities in Moscow and away from market considerations. In practice, of course, there was significant slackness in the control which the central planners were able to exercise. The technical means were not available that would have enabled them to exercise continuing close control over all aspects of a rapidly growing economy like that in the USSR. As a result, lower-level economic managers did have a degree of autonomy from the centre that is not reflected in the official organisational flow charts of the economy. Nevertheless the principle was clear: economic decisions were to be coordinated in an overall planning process which gave ultimate control to central planners and left no room for market prices. Within a very short space of time, what had been perceived as being the central motor force of economic development, the market, was rejected and replaced by a completely different principle, that of central direction. The administered, command or planned economy (all names were used) was created.

The Stalinist economic system is important not only because of the features of the system that was established, but also because of the means whereby it was created. It is clear that a significant level of coercion was used. This was most evident during the course of collectivisation, when at times military means had to be used to suppress peasant opposition. But it was also used in the industrial workforce, principally in the form of harsh legislation designed to establish labour discipline and to tie workers to their existing jobs. The rapid expansion of industry created labour shortages which meant that factory managers were unable to use unemployment and its threat as a means of labour discipline. This role could be played only by legislation, and this was put in place early in the 1930s: in January 1931 violators of labour discipline were made subject to imprisonment; in February 1931 workbooks were introduced for industrial and transport workers; in August 1932 the death sentence was introduced for the theft of state or collective farm property; in November 1932 a day's absence from work could mean dismissal; and in December 1932 internal passports were introduced, thereby regulating the movement of labour. Through this web of legislation, the state sought (with less than total success) to control the urban labour force, just as it controlled the peasants through their membership of the collective farms. Another aspect of this reliance upon

20

coercion was the use of prison labour. Many of the major development projects at this time, including the White Sea–Baltic Canal opened in July 1933 and the Moscow–Volga Canal opened in July 1937, were constructed largely by the forced labour of prisoners. The use of mass coercion at this time for the achievement of political aims provided both a justification and a precedent for its use later, particularly because it was in these instances deemed to be successful.

But it would be wrong to attribute the massive economic changes solely to coercion. A major input into economic transformation was popular enthusiasm. In the countryside, most peasants were not enthusiastic about the changes, although even here there is likely to have been some support from among the poorest sections of the villages. However, among urban workers and many at middle-level positions in the economic structure, enthusiasm and support for the changes appear to have been quite strong. Many willingly worked overtime, throwing all of their energies into the effort to create a new society. The regime offered role models for these people, most spectacularly in the form of the Stakhanovite movement. This was a campaign designed to promote high levels of labour productivity, using as a model a coalminer, Alexei Stakhanov, who was credited with overfulfilling his work norm fourteen-fold. It was this enthusiasm which enabled many to ignore the socio-economic deprivation they had to endure in the new industrial slums that were the inevitable result of the rapid course of industrial growth. There was thus an enthusiastic response to the regime's efforts to mobilise the populace for its aims of economic transformation.

Much of the enthusiasm generated at this time was genuine. Among many, there seems to have been a real sense of excitement and of achievement, of building a brave new world in conditions that seemed unpropitious. Socialism as a way of life and the wave of the future seemed assured as the USSR surged forward at this time when the capitalist economies were wallowing in the trough of depression. The great transformation seemed to herald an end to the compromise with capitalism that NEP had clearly been, and a leap towards the achievement of those principles which, ultimately, lay at the heart of the regime's legitimacy. It was this conviction that they were building something new and worthwhile which stimulated the militant enthusiasm of this period. Although such enthusiasm may have dissipated in later years, it was clearly a feature of the First Five Year Plan period.

A significant effect of the attempt to mobilise all efforts into achieving the goals of economic transformation was the reduction in the conception of what constituted the private sphere of a citizen's life. The Shakhty affair in 1928 [9] was instrumental in this. A trial of mining engineers charged with sabotage and collusion with foreign powers, this had established the principle that there could be no neutrality in the struggle to build socialism. People either supported that aim or they opposed it, and if the latter, they could legitimately be suppressed. The elimination of the possibility of neutrality plus the demand that all assist the programme of transformation, effectively reduced the scope of what was perceived to be a legitimate private sphere of a citizen's life and politicised social relations. All had to contribute to the struggle for socialism, and therefore all areas of life were legitimate areas of concern for the state.

[ii] Cultural revolution

The mobilisation of all efforts for the achievement of regime goals was also to have an effect in the cultural sphere during the 1930s. In the period 1928–31, culture was dominated by proletarian values [26; 59]. During this period, called the cultural revolution, literature and art adopted radical postures in their concentration on the ordinary worker, with the cult of the small man in the ascendant. The heroes of socialist construction were the factory workers and the toiling peasants, as the main focus of culture was on the lower levels of the social structure. Notions of class struggle, so evident in the rhetoric accompanying the quest for economic transformation, intruded into the cultural sphere with the demand that all culture should embody proletarian values rather than those associated with the bourgeoisie. Indeed, the cultural revolution was aimed at establishing the hegemony of proletarian values; and along with this rejecting the dominance of bourgeois ideology and values. It was the Shakhty trial and its rejection of professional expertise as a qualification for positions of trust and responsibility, which stimulated this emphasis on the small man, the proletarian, as the key to socialism.

But the focus of cultural and intellectual life was soon shifted, principally as a result of intervention by Stalin [93; 188]. The dominant trend in culture became much more closely and stridently tied to the imperatives of socialist construction. The main catchcall of this instrumental approach to culture was the doctrine of socialist realism, introduced by Stalin's associate Zhdanov at the first congress of the new Union of Soviet Writers in April 1934. The essence of this doctrine was that all culture should contribute to the construction of socialism; it should be optimistic and happy, with the heroes and heroines successfully overcoming seemingly insurmountable odds to place another brick in the edifice that was to be socialism. Those writers and artists whose work did not contribute in this way, whose work had no relevance for the imperatives of socialist construction, were unable to get an airing.

But perhaps at least as important as this tying of cultural production to the broader task of building socialism was the shift in focus away from the small man and onto those higher up the social and power scale. The heroes of fiction were no longer only the shopfloor worker and the peasant behind the plough. As well as people like Stakhanovites and record-breaking aviators, the heroes were the factory foremen and managers, the chairmen of collective farms, party secretaries and military leaders; the office-holder and the expert replaced the crude workman as the main force of socialist construction. Proletarian figures remained important, but chiefly when they had escaped from their proletarian origins either by gaining a responsible office or by becoming a Stakhanovite. No longer were the bosses, the authority figures, decried. In place of the cult of the little man was the cult of the big man. Hierarchy and authority emerged to replace the egalitarianism of proletarian values. This sort of development in the cultural field was consistent with developments in the ideological realm and in the social sphere, both discussed below.

The new cultural emphasis on hierarchy and authority was clearly much more conservative than the ethos which had prevailed during the cultural revolution. The predominance of a more conservative approach reflects in part the dominating position which more conservative elements within the cultural intelligentsia were able to achieve in the early 1930s, but it also reflects the emergence of a new political class whose cultural tastes appear to have been much more conservative than those of their predecessors [60]. The newly emergent class saw no value in culture for its own sake, having instead a contempt for modern trends and a desire to preserve those values which they believed were useful for the task at hand, socialist construction. Moreover, consisting of upwardly mobile workers and peasants whose cultural experience and horizons were severely limited, this new class was unlikely to appreciate *avant garde* art and culture; their preferences were likely to turn to the more traditional, conservative values associated with a style of life characterised by order, routine, propriety and respectability [171]. This conservatism was also evident in public life. Egalitarianism was now rejected as inequality and privilege became positive concepts. Increasing wage differentials and material incentives were lauded for their positive effects on worker performance. Public morality became more unbending: emphasis was placed on motherhood and the traditional family structure, divorce was made difficult to obtain, free marriage was denied its former legal status, and abortion and homosexuality were made illegal. Conservatism dominated in the public sphere.

This was also evident in the symbolism of nationalism. The process of collectivisation was accompanied by the official clamping down on expressions of nationalist sentiment by political and cultural elites in the non-Russian areas of the USSR. 'Bourgeois nationalism' became unacceptable and grounds for purging. But the most spectacular side of this rejection of non-Russian nationalisms was the dramatic resurgence of Russian nationalism in the symbolism of the regime. Increasingly the touchstone of virtue became Russia, its history and culture. Symbols of the Russian past, including the leading figures of Russian state-building such as Peter the Great and Ivan the Terrible, soon became prominent in the regime's symbolic universe. Similarly reflecting the dominant emphasis on the big man, the heroes who had saved Russia from foreign enemies in the past, such as Nevsky, Suvorov and Kutuzov, once again bestrode the stage like colossi. The wholesale rewriting of history proceeded apace. During this process of historical revision, the pasts of the non-Russian peoples of the USSR were rewritten in such a way as to present the Russians as their saviours. Russian traditions were restored in many walks of life. Russian nationalism became during this decade a principal ideological prop for the regime.

The prominence Russian nationalism achieved at this time in part reflects its manipulation by the central political authorities. The downplaying of cultural diversity which this implied fitted in well with the increased political control that stemmed from collectivisation and the spread of conservative values through the cultural sphere. All of these served to eliminate diversity and to channel all efforts into the drive for economic development. The emphasis on Russian nationalism played a part here also; its focus on the achievements of that national group whose levels of economic and cultural development were considered superior to those of the other national groups in the USSR, provided a stimulant for development. This use of Russian nationalism did not fall on deaf ears. It was a potent symbol for those millions of Russians who threw their efforts into the development plans, providing them with an important source of cultural identification, although its impact upon the non-Russian nationalities is likely to have been more problematic.

Similar trends were evident in the sphere of party ideology. Beginning in December 1929, the cult of Stalin had gradually spread until, by midway through the decade, it dominated the party's symbolic universe. Stalin was presented as omniscient and omnipresent; all the achievements of the regime were attributed to his genius, guidance and leadership, while his involvement and direction were a guarantee of success in any endeavour. Beginning in 1929, he was presented as the source of orthodoxy in ideological, cultural and intellectual matters [73; 188]. The indispensable role played by Stalin throughout the party's history was codified in what became the handbook of party history produced in 1938, the *History of the Communist Party of the Soviet Union (Bolsheviks). Short Course* [88]. The effect of projecting Stalin as the source of orthodoxy was to suck the life out of the ideology. It became a stale, formalised, stylised set of formulae used to justify the official line. A good example of this was Stalin's declaration that, the closer socialism approached, the greater was the opposition mounted to this and therefore the stronger the state had to be. With the growth of Stalinist authority through the cult, Marxism-Leninism became a rigid but subordinate element of public political life.

[iii] Social mobility

The conservatism in the cultural sphere contrasts starkly with the radicalism evident in the social sphere. During the 1930s, a social revolution of gigantic proportions took place [65; 66]. Large numbers of people suffered a significant loss of status and position at this time: those charged with being *kulaks*, many former owners, managers and 'bourgeois specialists' in industry, and those who were caught up in the purges during the second half of the decade, all suffered in this way. But this downward move of groups was more than balanced by the massive dimensions of the upward mobility experienced by members of the working class and peasantry. One of the principal effects of the 'revolution from above' was to open up opportunities for people to move into new, higher status jobs. In the countryside, collectivisation created a need for large numbers of officials to run the new rural organisations, and although many of these new posts were initially filled from among urban inhabitants mobilised into the countryside, many also were filled from among the peasantry. But more important was industrialisation. As increasing numbers of factories opened up, the demand for labour increased dramatically. Millions of peasants flooded into the towns seeking employment in these factories, thereby setting their feet firmly on the first rung of the newly developing social ladder; between 1926 and 1939, the proportion of the population that lived in the urban areas increased from 18 to 33 per cent. Despite the appalling conditions people had to endure, living in slums on the outskirts of the cities, poorly served by public transport and social services, and working long hours in what were often dangerous and unhygienic conditions, the move to the cities appears to have been seen in a positive light because it opened up far more opportunities for advancement than were available in the countryside. Those who showed any initiative or skill were likely to gain quick promotion to foremen or managerial positions because here too the demand outstripped the supply.

An important aspect of this process of upward social mobility was the expansion of education that was sponsored at this time [61; 67]. Prompted by the desire to replace the bourgeois specialists by those trained under Soviet auspices (a desire stimulated by the Shakhty trial), beginning in the late 1920s intensive efforts were made to expand facilities for technical education and to direct large numbers of young people into them. The effect of this drive for increased education was to ensure that throughout this decade, large numbers of people better educated than their parents were entering the workforce. Moreover they possessed a Soviet education rather than one provided by the old regime. Some figures will illustrate the dimensions of this process. In 1926–7, the total number of students in secondary higher schools was 1,834,260; by 1933–4 this had increased to 5,940,569, and by 1938–9, to 12,088,772 [61: 238]. In all higher educational institutions, the number of students increased from 159,800 in 1927–8 to 469,800 in 1932–3, with the proportion coming from the working class increasing from 25.8 to 50.3 per cent over this period [61: *188*]. Graduation rates escalated, with 170,000 graduating from higher education institutions (excluding military institutions) between 1928 and 1932, and 370,000 between 1933 and 1937. Promotion was rapid; by 1941, 89 per cent of the 1928–32 graduates and 72 per cent of the 1933–7 graduates were leading cadres. A whole new class moved into positions of dominance throughout the society.

Another major source of social mobility was the purges. For every person who was removed from a responsible post, another had to be found to fill that post. There has been considerable debate, much of it of a technical, statistical nature, about the number of casualties in the purges. All estimates are based on partial or incomplete statistical sources, and therefore all must be treated with caution; estimates have ranged from the hundreds of thousands to about 15 million, with observers divided, often bitterly, over the scale of repression. The partial opening of the archives has not resolved this issue, although those who have gained access to them seem to agree that the figure is much higher than the low figure cited above but substantially less than the 15 million; it may have been somewhere near 5 million. It is clear that the casualties were substantial, directly affecting all families in the USSR. Casualties were particularly high among those occupying high office in all of the major sectors of life, whether political (although Stalin's immediate entourage was an exception), economic, social, military or cultural [32; 33; 67; 128; 175]; for example, among the political elite, according to Khrushchev, 70 per cent of the party Central Committee were arrested and shot [96: *37*]. As a result, by the end of the decade the Soviet elite was probably the youngest and the most humble in its social origins of any elite which ruled any major country – in 1939, the average age of Politburo members was 50.3, of full Central Committee members 43.7, and of members of the Presidium of the Council of Ministers (the cabinet) 42.2 [17: *89*]. The aim of the October revolution had been to put the proletariat in power, and by 1939 most of the positions of authority in the USSR were filled by those whose social origins were either working class or peasant. The social revolution which these levels of social mobility constitute clearly is as great in its importance as the political revolution of 1917. It was the people who gained advancement at this time who would lead the Soviet Union into the 1980s.

If the economic, cultural and social faces of Stalinism emerged at the time of the 'revolution from above' at the beginning of the 1930s, the political face did not appear until the end of the decade. It was the great terror of 1936–8 which ushered the essential aspects of Stalinist politics onto the Soviet stage.

[iv] The great terror

One important theme which developed during the 'revolution from above' and which was important in facilitating the purges was the search for enemies. The insecurity evident during the earlier period and reflected in the distrust of NEP remained a significant theme within party life. Concern at the alien influence and the possible infection of the proletarian party and regime by the petty bourgeois peasantry was an element which made collectivisation popular among many party members. This concern was joined about the time of collectivisation by worries about the reliability of specialists employed in the economic structure. Between 1928 and 1934, these worries were reflected in a series of trials of specialists in the economy: the Shakhty engineers, the 'industrial party', the Mensheviks, the state farm and Agriculture Commissariat officials, and the Metro-Vickers engineers [9; 128; 179]. The trend was set by the Shakhty trial in 1928 which sought to link the domestic class enemy with the hostile capitalist powers and to cast suspicion over the reliability of all technical experts working in the economy. This stimulated the training of Soviet experts and politicised all social relations. It also helped to embed the notion of hidden enemies even deeper into the party's psyche.

This notion was extended, paradoxically, during the successful collectivisation campaign [73; 75]. Many local party leaders, those charged with the actual implementation of the party's policy, were unhappy with that policy, or at least with the speed and vigour with which it was being applied. These are the people who were criticised for soft-pedalling the policy in the countryside in Stalin's famous 'Dizzy with Success' article in March 1930 [177, vol.12: *197–205*]. The importance of this is that it transferred the notion of enemies into the party's ranks. This was confirmed when the party purge of 1933–4 was announced, and among those groups who were to be excluded were double-dealers who deceived the party and sought to undermine its policy, those who discredited state and party decisions by questioning their practicability, and 'enemies with a party card in their pockets'. While this purge did aim at general housekeeping tasks within the party, it is mistaken to argue, as Getty does [70; 71], that it did not also aim at eliminating enemies within party ranks. It is clear that in the central leaders' minds, at least part of the administrative sloppiness was due to the activities of those in the party who were opposed to the party and its policies. The purge's inability to rid the party of enemies is reflected in subsequent party policy. Particularly important were the campaigns for the verification of party documents in 1935 and the exchange of party cards in 1936. Like the earlier purge, both campaigns were directed in part at improving the party's administrative procedures, but in their intent and implementation they were directed at those who did not obey directions from the centre. These were seen as enemies, seeking to subvert party policy. The assumption that enemies of the party and the regime could be found inside the party was an important element which facilitated the outbreak of the great terror and the application of it to the party.

But recognition of this possibility alone was insufficient to break down the party's defences against such an attack upon it as an institution. What was important was the power which the leader, Stalin, was able to accumulate and how he sought to use it. Plumbing the depths of an individual's personality is a risky business at the best of times, but it is even more so when there are no scientific records which would provide an insight into Stalin's state of mind. Explanations for the subsequent course of development which rely excessively upon assumptions about Stalin's mental illness should be treated with caution. It is, nevertheless, impossible to exclude the figure of Stalin from any explanation of developments in the 1930s.

At a minimum it can be argued that Stalin was concerned about his position at the beginning of the 1930s. In 1929 he was still a member of the oligarchy which ran the country, albeit the most important member. However, he was not in a position whereby he could ensure that his views held sway over those of his colleagues. Furthermore his position in the leading ranks of the party may have been weakened by the course of collectivisation. Although it had ultimately been successful, in its implementation it had been a close run thing and may have called his judgement into question in the minds of his leadership colleagues. Uneasiness over Stalin's leadership is reflected in the emergence of three shadowy opposition groups in the early 1930s: the Syrtsov–Lominadze group in 1930 and the Riutin Platform and the Eismont–Tolmachev–Smirnov group in 1932. The most important was the Riutin Platform which both criticised the collectivisation policy and called for the removal of Stalin. According to some accounts [138], Stalin called for the execution of Riutin but was overruled by a majority in the Politburo. If true, this showed the limits of his authority. The limits of his ability to get rid of his critics were further emphasised by the failure of the 1933–4 purge to remove those critical of the policies associated with his name, most importantly collectivisation. In addition, there was opposition to Stalin at the XVII Congress in January 1934, the so-called 'Congress of Victors', where in an unprecedented demonstration of independence and opposition 270 delegates (22 per cent of full delegates; according to another author the number was 300 [259: *200*] compared with three voting against Kirov) voted against Stalin in the election for the Central Committee. This was the first time since the early 1920s that large numbers of delegates had voted against an official candidate in a leadership election. All of this suggests a Stalin who was nowhere near as secure in his leading position as he would have wished.

This picture of a Stalin who saw his position as under threat provides a perfect backdrop for those theories which portray Stalin as the *eminence grise* behind the assassination of Leningrad party boss Sergei Kirov in December 1934 [138; also 70: *207–10*]. In these theories, Kirov is portrayed as the most likely alternative leader to Stalin, the person those who voted against Stalin at the XVII Congress preferred to see as party leader. Stalin is shown as wanting Kirov out of the way to remove the potential challenge. He is also shown as seeing Kirov's assassination as a means of legitimising the introduction of the terror, which he wanted to do in order to eliminate the opposition to him which he had been unable to remove through the 1933–4 purge. The insecure Stalin is thus shown as planning the terror of 1936–8 well in advance and plotting the Kirov assassination to provide a justification for this. This circumstantial case is plausible, but unproved; the Soviet archives have thus far produced no material that will either confirm or refute such an interpretation. However, an argument could also be mounted to the effect that the assassination was the work of the security apparatus, the NKVD. This body was anxious to make a strong case for its indispensability in the face of apparent challenges to it at this time; the moderation of domestic policy in 1933–4 (with the consequent downplaying of rhetoric about enemies in society at large – in contrast to the continuing search for enemies in the party) plus the reorganisation of the security forces in 1934 which seemed designed to restrict their capacity for independent activity, suggest a downgrading of the security apparatus. What better than the assassination or attempted assassination of a prominent party leader to emphasise the indispensability of the security forces? This argument too is plausible and has received some indirect support in the Soviet press through the charge that the assassination was plotted by NKVD chief Yagoda, but it remains unproved. But in any case, what is clear is that Stalin used the assassination to ram through legislation which made the unleashing of the terror easier.

Stalin introduced an 'extraordinary law' which denied those accused of terrorism any protection in the investigation of the charges, while that investigation was to be completed in the shortest possible time and immediately followed by execution of those found guilty. For the first time in the history of the party, party membership was not a barrier against the application of the death penalty. During the height of the terror, 1936–8, the security police could intervene at will in party affairs, removing party members for trial and execution without the prior permission of party authorities. The special place of the party in the structure of the regime was thereby removed [73]. Thus although the terror did not flow on immediately from the Kirov murder, this was important for the former's development; it both stimulated the hunt for enemies inside the party and provided the occasion for the introduction of measures which undermined the party's impermeability to the blows of the security police.

Like collectivisation which had preceded it, the terror was a searing experience for Soviet society. Untold numbers suffered, with only some of the most prominent appearing in the three show trials in Moscow in 1936, 1937 and 1938 [151; 152; 153]. These trials saw the discrediting of many of Stalin's former leading opponents, including Zinoviev, Kamenev, Piatakov, Radek, Bukharin and Rykov, all of whom were found guilty of fantastic charges and executed. The turnover in responsible positions at all levels of society was substantial, with the effect of destroying all of the institutional structures

31

of society as autonomous entities. The party and state machines, the trade unions, the youth league, even the military ceased to have an independent identity of their own; all were subject to the depredations of the security police and all lost substantial sections of both their leaderships and their rank-and-file members. Even the security police were not immune. When Stalin chose, the police were themselves purged, once in 1936 and again in 1938. It is clear that the police were operating under his general oversight, and while he did not know about every single person who was purged, the responsibility for the extent of the suffering ultimately belongs to Stalin because, at the least, he allowed it to happen. In fact, his complicity goes much further (see Chapter 4), and he must bear the moral responsibility for the enormous suffering the terror involved.

However, acknowledgement of Stalin's ultimate responsibility explains neither why the terror was instituted nor its scope. Both questions remain a matter of considerable debate. With regard to the former, the interests of both Stalin personally and the NKVD institutionally must be taken into account. For Stalin, the unleashing of police action appears to have been an attempt to use extraordinary measures to get rid of those opponents he had been unable to eliminate through the 1933–4 purge, the 1935 verification and the 1936 exchange. It may also have been a way of expunging the shadow of Trotsky (who was the indirect defendant in the show trials) from the Soviet landscape [259: 260–1]. For the NKVD, an expansion in their role in this way would have been very welcome had they felt under pressure as suggested above; not only did they gain a higher profile through the search for enemies, but they were also in the position to be able to take action against those who wished to see them downgraded, and through the emasculation of the party, to emerge as the leading institution in the Soviet system.

But motives like these are not sufficient to explain the scope of the terror. One element in this was the target-fulfilment mentality. All security forces had to achieve ever-increasing targets of arrests; failure to achieve targets rendered people subject to suspicion as enemies. The effect of this was compounded by inertia. Once the terror had begun, it gained its own momentum, as a result both of institutional rationale and of the mechanism of denunciation. If the rationale of the NKVD was perceived to be the uncovering of enemies, only if it was doing this could its existence be justified. This was reinforced by its desire to crush all institutional challengers to its primacy. But relevant too was the mechanism of denunciation; investigations proceeded in part through the extraction of confessions and the denunciation of others. Many people hoped to gain leniency for themselves or their families by cooperating with the NKVD, and were therefore willing to denounce others to the security organs. The circle of victims thereby widened. Local initiative, in the form of people using the terror to deal with their own enemies, may also have been important in determining the terror's extent.

[v] Stalinist politics

If the reasons for the terror and its scope are still under debate, there is no disagreement about its effect. The terror ushered in a new form of political system in the Soviet Union, the Stalinist system. This was a system in which the personal dictator was supreme. His will was law, and henceforth no one openly challenged his authority; if in the early 1930s Politburo members disagreed with Stalin, and there was some opposition to the terror at the February–March 1937 CC plenum, from 1938 people generally accepted what Stalin said as their own views [209: *43 & 50*]. No longer was Stalin simply the most important cog in an oligarchy; now he was the focus and major power in the leadership. He could decide issues as he wished, without the fear that he would be overturned.

But personal dictatorship alone does not constitute a Stalinist political system. The other central aspect of the system was the institutionalisation of the terror. By unleashing the terror on the party during the 1936–8 period, Stalin both reinforced the politicisation of all social relations and entrenched uncertainty into the operating principles of the system. The rules of politics had now changed; opposition could mean death, so that the stakes for political players were much higher. This constituted a fundamental change from the system which went before and, in conjunction with the personal dictatorship, clearly marks the Stalinist political system dating from the end of the 1930s as fundamentally different from any which had preceded it.

However, the centralisation of political affairs which the dominance of Stalin represents does not mean that central controls over lower-level figures were tight and continuing. Regional leaders retained substantial autonomy in local affairs, albeit within a framework in which the centre could remove those leaders if it wished. But the institutional machinery for exercising close, continuing control was lacking. Local party leaders were still able to follow substantially their own policy lines in local affairs; the levying of their own local taxes on top of central demands is one illustration of the room for manoeuvre they possessed. Furthermore the degree of control which local party organs themselves were able to exercise over their local regions remained limited by such things as poor transport and communications, despite the effects of the 'revolution from above'. The high level of centralisation at elite levels thus coexisted with significant looseness lower down the political structure. The cult of Stalin may in part have been a means of seeking to overcome this organisational weakness by creating a structure of authority based on symbolism rather than organisation. The Soviet system clearly did not match the totalitarian model which has often been used to analyse the USSR, although it was powerful enough and its organisational sinews were sufficiently strong to maintain its dominance within Soviet society.

The economic, cultural and social faces of Stalinism thus emerged at the beginning of the 1930s. The political face emerged at the end of that decade. One scholar has argued that the economic crisis of 1927–8 was the midwife of Stalinism [148]. Clearly the economic difficulties at the end of the 1920s were central to the introduction of those policies which constituted the 'revolution from above'. They were therefore important for the economic face of Stalinism and, to the extent that both the cultural and social faces flowed from the 'revolution from above', for those faces as well. But the consolidation of these faces in the Soviet landscape did not predetermine the political face of Stalinism. The regime could have remained highly mobilisational in nature, characterised by those features which constituted the economic, cultural and social faces of Stalinism without adopting the political face and the personal dictatorship and institutionalisation of terror that this involved. The terror, and the consequent establishment of the political face of Stalinism, did not grow automatically from the 'revolution from above', as the relaxation in domestic policy in 1933–4 demonstrates. Certainly the 'revolution from above' facilitated the later terror; it stimulated the concerns about enemies inside the party and it legitimised the use of coercion to achieve political goals, but it was not intrinsically part of the same process [166; 192], except in the broadest sense of giving

34

rise to the Stalinist phenomenon. The terror was instituted by political decisions in the latter half of the 1930s that were designed to cope with what those who made those decisions perceived to be problems. While those problems may in part have been due to the 'revolution from above', this was not their sole source. There was, therefore, no necessary generative link between the 'revolution from above' and the terror, between the economic and political faces of Stalinism.

[vi] A foreign threat?

The emergence of the four faces of Stalinism during the 1930s was a result primarily of domestic Soviet factors. However it also took place against a background of perceived foreign threat. Note has already been made of the 1927 war scare and the fears about internal enemies linking up with foreign enemies to challenge the regime. While there is no evidence that such a development was likely, the international scene remained one of almost unremitting hostility to the Soviet Union. The leading Western powers remained hostile to the Soviet Union and its support for world revolution, especially when the Western system itself seemed to be vulnerable during the depression. Following this, the growth of fascism, marked most importantly by the rise of Hitler in Germany but also by Italian expansion in Africa and the civil war in Spain, made the international scene appear even more inhospitable for Moscow than it had before. Japanese expansionism in China and most importantly the clash with Soviet troops at Khalkin Gol in 1939, seemed to presage a sharpening of anti-Soviet tensions in the East. To the extent that the Stalinist faces were a response to the fear of enemies, enemies in the international arena were also relevant.

3 The War and High Stalinism

By the end of the 1930s, Stalinism was a rounded system, with all four faces established. This does not mean that further development and change were not possible, but that the changes that did occur took place within the boundaries previously established. An important stimulus in this process was provided by the war.

[i] The wartime economy

The Stalinist economic system was one well suited to the war effort. Indeed, the economies of many of the other combatants moved in the direction of greater central coordination and planning, like that associated with the Soviet economic structure created during the 1930s. The centralisation of control meant that the economy could quickly move onto a full war footing, particularly since the last years of the 1930s had seen an increasing emphasis placed upon the production of weapons and war materiel in general. In this sense, the general priority on heavy industry evident in the earlier decade was also useful for the war effort because it facilitated the move to wartime production much more than would have been the case had a focus on light industry and consumer goods production been characteristic of the Soviet development pattern.

The dangers to national survival, reflected most starkly in the advance of the German army to the gates of Moscow, instilled a sense of purpose and urgency which helped propel economic decision-making in a more centralised direction. The institutional manifestation of this was the establishment of the State Defence Committee on 30 June 1941, some eight days after the German invasion. This body formally had absolute power over all other organisations in the country, including party, state and military organs, and was the supreme authority on all matters. Headed by Stalin, in his new position of Chairman of the Council of People's Commissars, or prime minister, the State Defence Committee was the focus of all high-level Soviet activity on the economic front.

The economic priorities of the pre-war period were also reaffirmed during the war, at least in the sense that consumer goods remained a very low priority for the Soviet authorities. All efforts were mobilised for the war, with even greater controls being placed on all aspects of economic development; quarterly and even monthly plans were introduced in an attempt to further the war effort. By 1942 some 55 per cent of the national income was devoted to 'military purposes', a proportion that was reflected in a significant expansion of military production; in 1942 the USSR produced 60 per cent more aircraft and 3.7 times more tanks than it had in 1941 [139: 273]. The priority given to the war effort thus left very little room for the provision of consumer goods, with only 14 per cent of the cloth, 10 per cent of the clothing, 16 per cent of the knitwear and 7 per cent of the footwear available for sale in 1943 as there had been in 1940 [139: 278]. This economic performance was impressive, especially given the substantial loss of productive capacity associated with the German invasion. Food supply was also disrupted, leading to difficulties in some areas; in 1943 bad harvests were partly alleviated by American imports, but not enough to avoid famine in parts of Kazakhstan in 1944.

The mobilisation of all resources for the war effort meant a further tightening of discipline in the factories and on the farms. The amount of labour individual farmers had to contribute to the collective farms was increased in 1942, while disciplinary measures introduced into the factories in 1940 were extended. Workers in the war industries and transport were placed under military discipline; voluntary resignation was not permitted, overtime was made compulsory, holidays abolished, and the mobilisation of those not engaged in essential areas was instituted. Such disciplinary measures were buttressed by a surge of patriotic enthusiasm as the population rallied to defend the Motherland against the attack from without.

The patriotism which surged at this time, reflecting the instinctive reaction to the German invasion, repulsion at the ferocity of the German treatment of occupied areas and the stimulus of Soviet propaganda, was also important in reinforcing the ties of authority which bound the economic structure together. Despite the formal centralisation of authority in the State Defence Committee, the channels through which such authority could be exercised over the lower-level components of the economic machine remained underdeveloped. Lower-level economic leaders retained considerable practical autonomy in the running of their affairs. The mechanisms that would have enabled continuing central monitoring of performance were not in place, while the proliferation of instructions from above and the contradictory nature of the directives and goals often contained in them meant that lower-level functionaries possessed room for manoeuvre that made the economic machine much less centralised than it appeared. Indeed, the growth of private plots on the outskirts of the cities in an endeavour to meet the food shortages reflects the way in which the high level of centralisation was accompanied by significant practical looseness. The commitment of all to the war effort and the associated power of patriotism helped to prevent the system from breaking down under the pressures posed by the war.

[ii] Cultural mobilisation

Patriotism was also important in the growth of the cultural face of Stalinism during the war. The most important aspect of the development of Stalinist culture at this time was the growth of Russian nationalism. This aspect of cultural life had been quite prominent since the mid-1930s, but during the war it came to dominate the entire Soviet symbolic universe. The historic defenders of the Russian Motherland were projected through all avenues of cultural expression from war propaganda to literature, the theatre, education, art and the cinema. The building of the Russian state and its defence against aggressors became continuing themes as the current struggle was rooted into Russian historical consciousness. Much was made of the defence of Moscow, the traditional capital, in these terms. The Orthodox Church, vigorously repressed during the 1930s, was restored to official favour, and all of the symbolism that was associated with it was directed into the defence of the Motherland.

The appeal to Russian nationalism was profoundly conservative. It constituted a falling back on the traditions and culture heroes of the past of much of the Soviet population. But it was also exclusionist. In the face of this emphasis upon Russian culture and values, the cultures of the non-Russian nationalities were downgraded significantly. A programme of Russification was maintained, as the highest ideal appeared to be the Russian identity. The contempt with which the other national groups were treated is illustrated by the fate of eight small national groups (the Karachai, Kalmyk, Chechen, Ingush, Balkar, Volga German, Crimean Tartar and Meshkhetian Turks) charged with aiding the Germans. They were deported from their homelands to Siberia and Kazakhstan in late 1943–early 1944 [36]. Within the outflowing of Russian nationalism, the non-Russian nationalities appeared as minor social groups whose present state of development and current advances had been due solely to the leadership of the Russians.

An important aspect of this emphasis upon the Russian past was the way in which the cult of Stalin was associated with the historic figures of Russian tradition. Cast in the mould of the tsar defenders of Russia, Stalin was projected as the great war leader. Despite parts of the government being evacuated to Kuibyshev on the Volga, Stalin rarely left the Kremlin, except to travel to his dacha on the outskirts of Moscow. Pictures were prepared and displayed showing Stalin at the front (although in fact he appears only to have approached the front lines on one occasion, in August 1943, when he did little more than have his picture taken), while Soviet soldiers were encouraged to run into battle crying 'For Stalin! For the Motherland'. Symbolically, Stalin represented the link between the successes achieved by the former great leaders of Russia and the current struggle against the Germans. He was the new tsar, the defender of holy Russia.

Another important aspect of the cultural face of Stalinism was the decline in the role of Marxism-Leninism. This was overwhelmed by the patriotic emphasis, and is symbolised by the speech delivered by Stalin on 3 July 1941 when he summoned the Soviet people to struggle for victory over the invading forces. This speech, which was his first public response to the German invasion, was completely devoid of the symbolism and rhetoric of the building of socialism, and this remained a characteristic of Soviet public life throughout the war. Indeed, the formal ideology of the regime virtually ceased to be a feature of the regime's relationship with its citizenry; rampant Russian nationalism replaced it as the most important form of public discourse.

Change also occurred in the content of such cultural vehicles as literature, art and the cinema, although the essence of the message remained unchanged. If in the 1930s, Soviet cultural figures had been encouraged to focus on the struggle for the building of socialism, during the war the overwhelming emphasis was upon achieving military victory. The worker in the factory and the peasant on the land were now joined by the soldier in the trenches as fighters for the regime's ends. Culture was still seen in an instrumental fashion; its task was to contribute to the overall aim of the society, and this shift from socialist construction to military victory did not change this goal-related task. However, within these parameters there was greater freedom about what could be produced in the cultural sphere than there had been in the 1930s. Political controls were relaxed in an endeavour to stimulate enthusiasm for the war effort, resulting in a degree of flexibility in the cultural sphere unknown since the 1920s.

The conservatism evident in the cultural realm during the 1930s therefore remained during the war, buttressed most especially by the heavy emphasis upon patriotism. In the realm of public morals it was evident also. The mobilisation of all energies for the war effort reinforced the earlier emphases upon discipline in the economic sphere. The values of the family and high moral rectitude retained an important place in the system of public values, although always within a context of commitment to the cause of winning the war. Virtue, self-sacrifice and heroism were the order of the day. Such a focus was particularly important because of the absence of so many men at the front, leaving their wives and loved ones at home to cope as best they could. These sorts of values were therefore important not just for the shaping of behaviour patterns within Soviet society, but also for the sake of the soldiers' peace of mind and therefore for the war effort.

[iii] The social face

Turning to the social face of Stalinism, the wartime experience was, like the 1930s, one of significant social mobility. Two major avenues operated at this time. The first was the army. The need for troops was almost unending, particularly in the light of the serious reverses suffered at the outbreak of hostilities. The longer the war continued, the longer the lists of casualties, with the consequent continuing need for ever more troops; by war's end, the Red Army comprised some 5 million men, while approximately another 8 million soldiers died during the war. Entry into the army was, for many people from the countryside, an important step along the path of social mobility. Armies have often played this role, taking in the uneducated, often providing them with a skill, and thereby better equipping them to make their way in civilian life. The Soviet army did this for many during the war, but even for those who did not gain skills that they could put to later civilian use, military service affected their social status; many remained in the high-status officer ranks, while for many others war service lifted them out of the rut into which they had settled in the pre-war period.

The other avenue of vast social mobility, the movement into major roles in the production process, principally affected women. With the draining of large numbers of men away to the war, and the continuing high demands for increased production in both the factories and the farms, the worker vacancy had to be filled by women and children. During the war, large numbers of women in particular moved into jobs which had previously been performed by men. The factory workforce had a significant infusion of female labour (during the war some 53 per cent of the urban workforce was female) while on the farms women also took over much of the heavy work which previously had been dominated by the men. By moving into more responsible and higher status positions, women in general appeared to be major winners in the social sphere. However, this was not to last beyond the peace.

[iv] Wartime politics

The effect of the war was to strengthen two of the strands that made up the political face of Stalinism – personal dictatorship and the autonomy of lower-level political actors. At the centre of the Stalinist system, Stalin's personal position was strengthened. With the revelations under 'glasnost' [232], it has become clear that earlier suggestions that Stalin had been immobilised by the German attack [e.g. 194: *540*] were wrong; although Stalin did not respond publicly to the outbreak of war until 3 July, some 11 days after the German invasion, he was very active in meetings and organisational work outside the public gaze. There is no question of his not playing a leading role at the centre of the war effort at any time during that conflict. His personal dominance was enhanced by the decline of the major institutional structures that had dominated Soviet politics before the Stalinist political system had come into being. As effective operating bodies, the central organs of the party ceased to operate. No party congress was convened during this period, the full CC plenum appears not to have met, and while the Politburo, Orgburo and Secretariat may have met on a more regular basis, they exercised little power. The leading state organ, the Council of People's Commissars, also played little role in government affairs. These major institutions were replaced by the State Defence Committee and by the military Supreme Command, or Stavka. These two bodies, linked by Stalin who headed them both, were the main institutional foci of central political life. The State Defence Committee was a new body, created by Stalin to handle the war, while the Stavka could play the sort of role it did only because Stalin had ushered it forward onto the national stage. Neither body was therefore in a position to impose any significant constraints upon Stalin, and in practice, much decision-making occurred informally in Stalin's office, even if the decisions were announced under the formal aegis of one of these bodies. Furthermore the security apparatus was still active, and this remained under the control of one of Stalin's closest supporters, Beria.

A further sign of the weakness of the party and state structures was that the distinctions that had been maintained between them effectively disappeared, at least at the centre where the leading bodies were fused. This is best illustrated by the way in which Stalin became Chairman of the Council of People's Commissars (or prime minister) in May 1941 while remaining party Secretary, and by the way in which members of the State Defence Committee took on responsibility for the major branches of production regardless of the offices they formally held in either party or state [166: 499].

While the reduction of the party and state machines in this way enhanced Stalin's position, this does not mean that he alone made decisions. Khrushchev's picture of Stalin deciding battle strategy on a globe of the world is clearly a caricature [16; 37; 96: 58]. Nevertheless Stalin's influence was predominant, especially in the early phases. He became involved in all manner of issues, including military strategy and tactics, supply, personnel and armaments production, often with disastrous results; the high level of Soviet losses on the battlefield may in part be due to his involvement in operational decision-making. Following the initial military setbacks, Stalin usually sought advice from the military experts, in particular Shaposhnikov, Zhukov, Vasilievsky and Antonov. Issues were discussed, and although all could have their say, ultimately Stalin was able to resolve the question in whichever way he thought fit. Nevertheless, following the initial period, Stalin relied heavily upon his military advisers, with many decisions being resolved without Stalin's personal involvement. This meant that there was always a struggle between Stalin's subordinates for his ear, with the result that Stalin's 'court' remained the scene of intrigue and factional struggle, albeit muted by the war, throughout this period. The origin of many of these struggles for the dictator's ear preceded the outbreak of the war and were the products of longstanding rivalries [85]. Many were not resolved until after hostilities had ended.

But if Stalin's personal power was consolidated during the war, so too was the practice of effective autonomy on the part of lower-level political actors which had existed during the 1930s. Although the security apparatus remained an instrument that the centre could use to bring recalcitrants into line, the weakness of the continuing linkages between the centre and lower levels posed a major barrier to the exercise of effective monitoring by Moscow. The concentration of efforts on the war and the overwhelming commitment to successful prosecution of it, meant that as long as the lower levels were seen to be contributing to that effort, they were likely to be left substantially to their own devices. There was thus no real change to central–lower-level relations; providing the latter did not bring unfavourable attention to themselves through poor performance, they would be left alone. Thus even during the war and the pressures for centralisation that that involved, the political system retained a high degree of effective decentralisation.

In May 1945, the German surrender brought the war in Europe to a victorious end for the Soviet Union and the Allied powers. Victory had been very expensive for the USSR; as many as 50 million Soviet soldiers and civilians may have been killed or incapacitated during the war [230: 218]. Many towns and cities lay in ruins, with almost half of all urban living space in occupied territory destroyed. Large numbers of factories were left in ruins, while much of the agricultural infrastructure was destroyed. The transport network in the occupied areas had to be almost totally rebuilt. But ultimately, the USSR had triumphed. The Stalinist system was partly responsible for this. While it is true that the midwife of political Stalinism, the terror, had contributed to the early setbacks suffered by Soviet forces, the centralisation of the economic and political structures enabled the transformation of the economy onto a war footing in a shorter time than would have been possible had the economy worked on a decentralised, market basis. Furthermore while the centralisation of political power magnified the effect of any mistakes Stalin made, it also enabled speedy decision-making and similarly magnified the effect of good decisions. Moreover the propaganda apparatus that was developed was also instrumental, particularly in terms of its effect of maintaining popular enthusiasm and commitment. Indeed, the war posed a major test of the Stalinist system, and it had come through that test well. The question now was whether it could make the transition easily back to a peacetime situation.

[v] The high Stalinist economy

In the post-war period, discipline remained the defining watchword of Soviet reality. Rather than the relaxation many had expected following the rigours of the war, the official emphasis was once again one of commitment and discipline. In the economic sphere, Stalin dismantled the institutional arrangements he had set in place during the war; the State Defence Committee was abolished and the Council of Ministers (which the Council of People's Commissars was renamed in 1946) re-emerged as the leading economic organ [52]. The task to be fulfilled was enormous: the very high level of economic destruction caused by the war had to be repaired, and because of the early growth of tension with the West, this had to be done overwhelmingly from domestic resources. There was a foreign input to this process in the form of the economic plant and materiel shipped back to the USSR from the Eastern European countries at the end of the war, but the vast bulk of the impetus for economic development came from within.

The priority for repairing the war damage plus the perception of a hostile West strengthened pressures for the maintenance of the economic model and its heavy industry priority that had emerged during the 1930s and been consolidated during the war. The directive nature of the economy was maintained, with all major economic goals set in the central planning agency in Moscow and passed down to the subordinate levels of the economic apparatus in the form of plan targets. In practice, of course, considerable local autonomy continued severely to qualify the extent of central direction. The primary emphasis remained the production of heavy industry and of those capital goods which were essential to the growth and development of the heavy industry sector. Consumer goods remained a low priority in the Stalinist development strategy; in the 1945–50 period, only 12.1 per cent of industrial investment was directed to the light and food industries, with the remainder going to the producer goods/heavy industry sector of the economy [139: *290*]. Planning goals remained taut, in the sense that high expectations were reflected in the plan targets adopted. Industry in the formerly occupied areas was rapidly rebuilt, with the 1940 production levels of coal, metallurgical output and electricity in Ukraine surpassed by 1950 [139: *239*]. The reconstruction effort, added to the increased capacity which had been developed in the Urals and Siberia during the war, ensured that by the time of Stalin's death the Soviet industrial infrastructure had recovered from the ravages of the war.

In the agricultural sector too there was an emphasis on the traditional Stalinist principles. In those areas which had been newly incorporated into the USSR, including the Baltic republics and parts of Poland and Bessarabia, agricultural land was collectivised and private agriculture as the principal form of farming eliminated [180]. Furthermore throughout the Soviet Union, new restrictions were placed upon the peasants' private plots. These had been given freer rein during the war, principally because of the parlous state the country found itself in, but in the post-war period policy turned once more to restricting these activities. Agriculture limped along, a product of the wartime devastation, drought in 1946, the official emphasis upon industrial development and a confused and misguided agricultural policy. A proliferation of bureaucratic controls over agriculture, the imposition of inappropriate cropping policies and the lack of adequate material or financial incentives all delayed agricultural revival. By 1952, the 1940 production levels in three main areas of the economy – grain, potatoes and cows – had still not been reached [139: *303*].

Mobilisation remained a major instrument of economic policy. Lacking sufficient resources of funds which could be directed into the manifold areas requiring capital investment, the authorities were forced to rely heavily on mobilising labour resources in pursuit of their economic goals. In overall terms there was no shortage of labour, although the toll taken by the war did reduce the numbers of men who, upon demobilisation, could enter the workforce. This meant that although when the men returned many women were forced out of the jobs they had taken on during the war, sections of the workforce remained much more heavily saturated by women than had been the case in the 1930s. Prison camp labour also continued to be used in industry, including importantly the nuclear industry.

But the problems with relying principally upon labour mobilisation for economic growth stemmed less from the number or gender of workers available than from the general feeling of exhaustion that afflicted the population as a whole. The physical demands of the war had sapped a lot of the energy out of the Soviet people, just as it had done for many of the other combatants, and although the first flush of enthusiasm with the victory helped to hide this fact, the attempts to rely on mass mobilisation brought it clearly to the fore. The results of relying upon this as the main economic mechanism were therefore disappointing from the leadership's perspective, and growth rates did not reach expected levels in all areas of the economy.

[vi] The social face

Levels of social mobility during this period seem to have been lower than they had been at earlier times. Many who had been in the army returned to take up factory jobs, and for many of these such employment was an improvement on what they had been doing prior to the war. The large numbers of men killed during the war also left gaps that had to be filled and therefore provided some additional scope for social mobility. However, as indicated above, the return of many men from the front forced large numbers of women out of the positions they had occupied in the workforce. For many, this involved a decline in the status of the jobs they performed, and therefore suggests a form of downward mobility on their part. But for many other women, their continuing role in the workforce meant improved education and an improvement in social status. Thus although there was some fluidity in the social sphere, the dimensions of this appear more limited than during earlier periods. The reduction in scope for mobility reflects a fundamental difference between the 1930s and this period: the rapid expansion of the economic mechanism compared with the struggle to get it back to what it had been before the devastation of the war.

For the ordinary populace, life remained difficult in the post-war period. The harshness and deprivation of the war years were eased, but the overwhelming concentration on the rebuilding of heavy industry meant that there was little scope for improvements in material standards of living. Housing remained in short supply, particularly in those regions that had been under wartime occupation, while the availability of consumer goods saw little improvement on the situation in the 1930s. Food supply also remained inadequate, with famine occurring in Ukraine in 1946; ration cards were not abolished until 1947. Thus as the Soviet people, like those of the other combatant countries, struggled to overcome the devastation wrought by the war, they continued to have to tighten their belts within an economy characterised by continuing scarcity.

[vii] Post-war culture

The cultural face of Stalinism remained dominated by a strongly conservative ethos. An important element of this remained Russian nationalism. Fuelled by the growing sense of hostility on the part of the outside world, reflected most graphically in the onset of the Cold War in the second half of the 1940s, official Russian nationalism became more chauvinistic and intolerant than it had been before. The glories of the Russian tradition were trumpeted across the length and breadth of the USSR. In accord with this, the traditions and cultures of the other national groups within the USSR were placed under extreme pressure as the drive for the Russification of these regions mounted. The chauvinism of this approach was reflected in the intolerance towards other cultures and values. This was illustrated most spectacularly by the bitter attacks on 'cosmopolitanism' towards the end of the 1940s and the claims that all of the most important discoveries, from the theory of relativity to the invention of the submarine, were made by Russians. Anti-semitism was particularly virulent.

In the field of public morality conservatism also held sway. This was particularly evident in the public attitude to women compared with men. Mention has already been made of the way in which women were expected to vacate their jobs in favour of men returning from the front. In the drive to make good the population losses sustained by the war, the official attitude became one of encouraging women to bear larger numbers of children; this was portrayed as their major, and patriotic, duty. Furthermore, reflecting the decline in the number of men and the consequent shortage of eligible bachelors to satisfy the number of women, men were made no longer legally responsible for children born out of wedlock. At the same time the family was a major positive symbolic element in the regime's set of values. Notions of women's rights, never a strong element under Stalinism, receded even further into the background in the post-war period. Abortion remained out of bounds and divorce was rendered very difficult to obtain.

This conservatism of the official value system was also evident in the emphasis upon status, hierarchy and differentiation. Within the cultural sphere, egalitarian principles rarely appeared; literature, art and the cinema all portrayed inequality, albeit based upon achievement and merit, in a positive light. Formal titles and ranks were restored in 1946 for workers in many spheres of life [140: *105*].

In art, literature, music and the cinema, a more conservative trend set in immediately after the war. Sponsored by Zhdanov, a drive was made to eliminate all alien elements from cultural life. All culture had to make a positive contribution to the construction of socialism, and in effect this meant the placing of a blanket of uniformity across all cultural production. Experimentation was denounced, as was servility to things foreign; cultural production had to reflect Russian nationalist sentiments and to eliminate all trace of things foreign [13; 43]. Indeed, cultural links with the outside world were almost severed at this point. The party hack replaced those with true imagination and ability, with composers like Shostakovich and Prokofiev being accused of a 'formalist' approach and a lack of party spirit.

The focus on party spirit also invaded other spheres. Disciplines like history, economics and philosophy had for a long time been under direct party control, with the party laying down the line which must prevail in each area. However, such control became much more constricting and inflexible during the post-war period. The most celebrated instance of this was in genetics, where the charlatan Trofim Lysenko was able to eliminate those who disagreed with him and to place his malign stamp upon the development of this subject in such a way as to divorce it completely from the path of development along which it was proceeding outside the USSR [92; 131]. Stalin's personal intervention in the field of linguistics in 1950 is another prominent example of this. The intellectual life of the country was clearly stunted by the assertion of intellectual orthodoxy over all fields of endeavour.

The rigidity of this control was matched by an increasing inflexibility in the ideological sphere. The ideology was very largely a set of formulae, devoid of any meaningful content. Despite some resurgence in the public realm following its demise during the war, under the hand of Stalin it had become an arid doctrine with little direct relation to reality. An important part of this doctrine, and one of the most important forces which enabled it to change, was the words of Stalin. Stalin's dominance in this sphere, reflected most spectacularly in the cult which now dominated the public symbolism of the regime, meant that whatever he said became doctrinal writ and therefore compulsory for all. It was this dominance more than anything else that reduced the ideology to the formalistic doctrine it had become.

[viii] The political face

Turning to the political face of Stalinism, the central component of this, Stalin's personal dominance, remained unshaken. Despite some resurgence of the party in the initial post-war years, sponsored initially by Zhdanov and then by Malenkov, both party and state organs remained subordinate elements in the political system. One party congress (October 1952) and one CC plenum (February 1947) met during this period, and although the executive organs of the CC may have met on a more frequent basis, real decision-making power did not lie in these bodies [17: *33*]. Decisions were made in informal groups of leaders which Stalin called arbitrarily to discuss various issues. These 'quintets', 'sextets' and 'septets' were *ad hoc,* convened at Stalin's whim, and played a purely advisory role [48; 96: *81*].

It would, however, be wrong to assume that there was no politics at the apex of the Stalinist system. The rivalries that had existed among Stalin's lieutenants continued to manifest themselves during this period. People such as Zhdanov, Malenkov, Khrushchev and Beria all struggled to gain the ear of the leader and to disparage their competitors. In doing so, and thereby in adopting different positions on policy issues, a variety of leaders engaged in clashes which fed into the decision-making process [82; 146]. But while such clashes may have helped to refine thinking on the issues at hand, and in some instances even to have determined the outcome of policy debate, this latter result occurred only when Stalin chose not to become directly involved. Certainly at different times during this period Stalin does seem to have been somewhat detached from the running of day-to-day affairs [51: *13–15;* 146: *179–80*]. But on those issues in which Stalin took an interest, he was able to decide the issue as he chose; his colleagues fell into line with his decision. Stalin was clearly supreme, at least at the decision-making level, and to say that his power was very limited [51: *146;* 120] is to miss the essence of his position and role.

The other central element of the Stalinist political system, the presence of terror, remained in evidence during this period. Institutionally reflected in the continuing high profile of the police throughout this period, and in particular police chief Beria's membership of the Politburo, terror remained a significant element in the public life of the USSR. The deportation of large numbers of citizens from the areas newly incorporated into the USSR and the forcible collectivisation of those areas, the incarceration in labour camps of those Soviet soldiers who had been taken prisoner by the Germans, the 'Leningrad Affair' of February 1949–October 1950 in which the leaders of the Leningrad political machine were dismissed and executed, the Mingrelian case of 1951–2 in which Beria's supporters in Georgia were purged, the 1952 Crimean case in which a number of prominent Jews were executed, and the 'Doctors' Plot' of 1952–3 in which leading doctors were accused of plotting the assassination of political leaders, all projected the police into a prominent place in the system. These cases made clear to all that the police machine was still in existence and could be wielded against them if they stepped out of line. As a buttress for Stalin's position, the police and the possibility of terror remained an important factor.

But just as in earlier periods, the high degree of centralisation of decision-making power in the person of Stalin was not matched by the ability of the central organs to exercise close continuing control over lower-level political organs. At the lower levels party and government leaders continued to exercise significant autonomy from the centre because no effective institutional mechanisms had been established binding the latter to the former. The centre could remove any lower-level leaders it wished, but it lacked the institutional means closely to monitor their day-to-day activity. The degree of centralisation thus remained more apparent than real, at least in the sense of continuing close supervision.

[ix] International Stalinism

The final aspect of Stalinism about which something should be said is its international dimension. During this period, Soviet control was extended over the countries of Eastern Europe and a fully-fledged system along Stalinist lines was imposed in each country [20; 173]. This does not represent some inherent imperial urge within Stalinism, nor does it reflect the inherent expansionist impetus of a Soviet or communist ethos. It reflects the political opportunity to establish control created by the driving back of German troops during the war, and the conviction on the part of Stalin that such a system was the best way of governing these states. An important part of this conviction was the realisation that the imposition of such a system would render Soviet control of these countries somewhat easier. The desire for such control seems to have been driven both by economic motives and, more importantly, by security considerations. In the immediate post-war period, the East European region was used as a source of resources for the economic rebuilding of the USSR. Industrial plant and materials were shipped as war reparations to the Soviet Union where they contributed to Soviet reconstruction. But of greater import was the desire to establish a buffer zone between the USSR and the West. The wartime harmony was seen as a temporary aberration, and the Soviet leadership realised that the country needed to be prepared for a post-war revival of tension. Soviet control over Eastern Europe was an attempt to build up the Soviet position in anticipation of the souring of relations with the West. The growth of tension in the second half of the 1940s confirmed Soviet fears and stimulated the consolidation of that control.

But the development of these Eastern European variants of Stalinism is not our concern here. Indeed, in the sense that each of these national systems was, ultimately, subordinate to Stalin himself, it can be questioned whether these constituted Stalinist systems in the same sense as that which applied in the USSR; Soviet national autarchy had no equivalent in these states.

51

4 The Nature of Stalinism

As the preceding discussion has suggested, Stalinism consisted of four distinct although related faces: the economic, the social, the cultural and the political. These did not come into existence at the same time, but sequentially, and it would therefore be wrong to see the Stalinist system as bursting forth fully developed at the time of the emergence of the first Stalinist faces during the 'revolution from above'. Care should therefore be taken in talking about the Stalinist system; fully fledged, it existed only from the end of the 1930s, flowing from the establishment of the Stalinist political system through the terror. The Stalinist economic system emerged at the beginning of the 1930s, while the cultural and social faces emerged at approximately the same time. In seeking to characterise Stalinism as a system, due regard must be paid to this sequential mode of its emergence and to the changing nature of the different faces which comprised it.

The essence of the economic face of Stalinism was an economic system which worked on the basis of directive principles rather than the operation of market forces. It was, therefore, a suitable instrument for the achievement of political aims. This is reflected both in the consistent priority given to the development of heavy industry and in the speed and relative ease with which it handled the transition to the demands of wartime. The emphasis upon heavy industry also meant an economy which paid little attention to the needs or demands of the consumers. In turn, this meant that there could be little reliance on material incentives to encourage the workforce; symbolic rewards were of much greater importance in a consumer-goods-deficit economy. This was a significant point in an economy which was extensive rather than intensive in its mode of development, relying upon increasing inputs of labour as an important stimulus to continuing economic growth. Mass mobilisation was therefore an important feature of this type of economic structure.

In its essentials, the Stalinist economic structure remained basically intact throughout the period from its establishment until Stalin's death. Its highly centralised, directive nature and considerable reliance on mass mobilisation characterised Soviet economic life throughout this period. There was, therefore, little structural change between the early 1930s and 1953. Growth rates throughout seem to have remained high, although they were publicly exaggerated and fluctuated much more than was acknowledged at the time, and there was a serious imbalance: rates of growth were much more impressive in the industrial sphere than in the agricultural, which throughout the period lagged significantly behind both the expectations of the leaders and industrial performance.

The chief characteristic of the social face of Stalinism during the 1930s was very high levels of social mobility. Reflecting the opportunities opened up by the 'revolution from above' and later by the terror, the 1930s witnessed a real social revolution in the USSR. Throughout the Soviet Union, members of the traditional lower classes moved into positions of power and privilege in all sectors of life. While in one sense this represented an urbanisation and embourgeoisement of the populace, in another it was the culmination of the political revolution of 1917. The old class structure based upon inheritance was demolished and a new social structure was emerging. This was anything but egalitarian, and privilege and prerogative seeped in as essential parts of the new structure, but for the vast mass of those upwardly mobile families, the revolution meant steps towards the realisation of aspirations to a more comfortable lifestyle. This social revolution, with the flow from the countryside into the towns and the percolation up into white-collar occupations of many of these new arrivals, transformed the society. Despite declining levels of mobility after the war, the overall impact was the substantial recasting of society. Changes in the class composition of Soviet society illustrate this transformation. According to Soviet sources the class composition of the society changed as follows (with some groups, such as the bourgeoisie, that disappeared in 1929–30 excluded from the 1924 figures):

	blue-collar workers (%)	peasants (%)	white-collar workers (%)
1924	10.4	76.7	4.4
1959	50.2	31.7	18.1

Even allowing for the general nature of the categories, the dimensions of this change are unprecedented within such a short space of 35 years.

The cultural face of Stalinism underwent a dramatic change in the early phase of its development. Initially the cultural revolution had sponsored values and beliefs which emphasised the egalitarian and the small man; the focus was upon the dominance of proletarian values and the way in which all aspects of cultural endeavour had to reflect those values. However, this changed in 1931, with a more conservative orientation entering the cultural sphere. The focus shifted away from the small man and onto those in leadership positions in all walks of life. Increased emphasis was placed upon the way in which culture was to be the handmaiden of socialist construction, how it was to contribute to the growth and development of a socialist society. In conjunction with this, egalitarianism was superseded as a positive value by rank, status and hierarchy. The new emphasis in literature on leaders and 'big men' was one aspect of this, but it was also reflected in the more general ethos of society which became much more conscious of and sensitive to considerations of rank.

But perhaps the most important manifestation of this more conservative direction in the cultural sphere was the emergence of Russian nationalism as a principal plank of the regime's legitimation programme. The early anti-national orientation of the revolution became in the 1930s subsumed under a wave of Russian nationalism which, in the extent of its development, became Russian chauvinism. The denial of the value of all other national traditions accompanied the glorification of the Russian past and its folk heroes as Stalinism became an almost entirely inward-looking cultural phenomenon. This was reflected graphically in the argument that international revolution could best be advanced by strengthening the USSR, a principle which justified the exercise of Soviet control over foreign communist parties.

The essential features of the political face of Stalinism remained in place throughout the post-1938 period in the USSR. The personal dictatorship whereby Stalin could decide anything he wished to decide regardless of the views of his fellow leaders was one such feature. This does not mean that Stalin decided all issues, but that those which he chose to decide were resolved by him. Although Stalin's active role in decision-making seems to have been much more limited after the war than just prior to and during it, this was a function of Stalin's choice, not of limits imposed upon him by others. What had created the conditions for such a centralisation of power was the terror, and what enabled that centralisation to be maintained was the continuing presence of the threat, and at times actuality, of the terror. Terror became an instrument of government in that it was a weapon which the dictator was able to use in order to root out opposition and to cow potential dissidence.

But the most important defining force within the system was Stalin himself; the contours of elite politics and the mode of operation of the entire system were moulded in accordance with his will and operated to fit in with his whim. Having eliminated all possible challenge to his position through the purges and prevented any resurgence of it through the ever present threat of terror, his personal position was rendered unassailable and the system was moulded to fit his preferences. Under such circumstances, the personality of the leader was bound to be very important for the system as a whole. It is difficult to disagree with the picture of Stalin as taciturn, intolerant and paranoid [174], unwilling to countenance anything which seemed to infringe upon his power or prerogatives. The arbitrariness of his actions reflects a confidence in the capacity of his power to achieve his ends, although the way it was used also suggests the suspicion of the motives and intentions of others which seems to have been such a feature of his career. Indeed, it is this combination of arbitrariness and suspicion which was the dominant element of his leadership style.

An important result of the personal dictatorship resting upon a terrorist basis was the excessive weakness of all political institutions. These were able to develop no integrity, autonomy or coherence; they could not act independently on the Soviet scene, nor could they structure their own internal operations. They were always subject to intervention and control by the leader. Institutional mechanisms were weakly developed. At the top, this meant that formal political organs were unable to exercise any control over the political leaders, as most clearly illustrated by Stalin's personal predominance. At lower levels too, the political organs could not exercise clear control over local political leaders who, frequently, were able to establish Stalin-like positions in their local areas. But this institutional weakness also meant that the central political bodies did not possess the means whereby they could establish close, continuing control over political organs at the lower levels. Central control was therefore episodic and much weaker than the model of a highly centralised Stalinist polity suggests. This characteristic was present throughout the life of Stalinism.

The changing nature of the four faces of Stalinism can be seen in terms of a radical-conservative dimension. All four faces became embedded in the Soviet landscape as a result of developments which were radical and revolutionary in nature; the smashing of the established structures at the time of the first five year plan and the physical elimination of large numbers of people in the terror. Furthermore, at the outset, all four faces were radical in nature, constituting both significant departures from what had gone before and new structures which reshaped those sectors of national life with which they were concerned. But the radicalism and the reshaping ceased, in the economic and cultural faces during the early 1930s, and in the social and political faces during the war. Henceforth the principal ethos within the faces of Stalinism was stabilisation and administration, not transformation, the management of what had been created rather than the building of a new world. This change from radicalism to conservatism was not something that was unique to Stalinism as a phenomenon. It was the inevitable result of the establishment of a structure of institutions and values and the inertia that results from such a structure once it is in place. Political will could have overcome that inertia, and there is some evidence that Stalin was planning this through the agency of another purge when he died, but in the absence of a concerted effort to disrupt the patterns that had developed, those patterns were likely to continue undisturbed.

This brief survey of the faces of Stalinism suggests that, as a phenomenon, it belies easy categorisation. Not only are many attempts at categorisation restrictive in the sense that they fail to encompass all the faces of Stalinism, but even with the more limited aim of taking account of only one face of Stalinism they often fail to recognise the changes that occurred within that face. For example, the application of the term 'revolution from above' [192] is clearly appropriate to the economic and cultural faces early in the 1930s, to the social face throughout the 1930s and perhaps to the political face towards the end of the 1930s, but it does not seem relevant to the cultural sphere for most of that decade nor for any face after the outbreak of the war. Neither does the view that Stalinism was a mass mobilising developmental dictatorship under single party auspices [80] fit well with the demise of the party or the economic aims of the post-war period. The characterisation of Stalinism as highly centralised can be applied to the decision-making process at the top of the Soviet hierarchy where Stalin's personal involvement was clearly immense, but it is less applicable when discussing the relations between central and lower-level political organs. Furthermore the term totalitarian, with its connotations of all-pervasive control, does not accord well with the severe limitations that existed on central power and the massive social upheavals over which it was physically impossible to exercise close control.

Recent scholarship has also raised another perspective on Stalinism, and one which has been widely criticised. Some social historians have focused their gaze overwhelmingly upon life at the lower levels of Soviet society [58; 64; 66; 70; 71; 117; 118; 161]. They have often consciously avoided Stalin and the national levels of politics, and in so doing have highlighted the chaos and uncertainty that prevailed at the lower levels of the Soviet system. This means that they have focused on the limits society, or perhaps better, the lower rungs of the political structure were able to impose upon the central political authorities. This sort of focus has been criticised on the grounds that it omits what is considered to be essential to an understanding of Stalinism, in particular the terror and the excessive centralisation of power in Stalin's hands and that it artificially minimises the capacity of the central authorities to affect developments at lower levels [29; 53; 94]. Such criticism is justified only in so far as those looking at the lower levels of society seek to make generalisations about the system in its entirety (including its upper levels) based only upon their view of the lower levels, or as they ignore the major impact the centre could and did have on life at the lower levels. It is legitimate to focus on non-central aspects of the system as long as the role of the centre is not artificially reduced or ignored. The main difference between these social historians and many of their critics is the direction from which they

57

have approached Stalinism, from below or above. Studies coming from either direction are valuable and legitimate and the conclusions they reach are likely to be different. But only a study which involves approaching from both directions can hope to be comprehensive.

All the characterisations noted above, along with a multitude of others, may capture one aspect of the Stalinist essence, but as characterisations of the phenomenon of Stalinism, they are clearly inadequate. No simple characterisation is possible because all four faces of Stalinism must be taken into account along with the developments that occurred within those faces. Keeping this in mind, we could construct a Stalinist syndrome along the following lines. Stalinism consisted of:

(i) a formally highly centralised, directive economic system characterised by mass mobilisation and an overriding priority on the development of heavy industry;

(ii) a social structure initially characterised by significant fluidity, most particularly in the form of high levels of social mobility which bring the former lower classes into positions of power and privilege; subsequent consolidation of the social structure results in the dominance of rank, status and hierarchy;

(iii) a cultural and intellectual sphere in which all elements are meant to serve the political aims laid down by the leadership and where all areas of cultural and intellectual production are politically monitored;

(iv) a personal dictatorship resting upon the use of terror as an instrument of rule and in which the political institutions are little more than the instrument of the dictator;

(v) all spheres of life are politicised, hence, within the scope of state concerns;

(vi) the centralisation of authority is paralleled by a significant measure of weakness of continuing central control, resulting in a system which, in practice, is in its daily operations loosely controlled and structured;

(vii) the initial revolutionary ethos is superseded by a profoundly conservative, status quo, orientation.

These are the elements which, in combination, constituted the Stalinist system.

[i] The origins question

A question which arises from this, and the question with which this book opened, is the source or origins of Stalinism. One of the most common lines of explanation, that associating the emergence of Stalinism with the backwardness and underdevelopment of Russia, has its origins in Stalin's defeated rival for power, Leon Trotsky. Although the precise details of Trotsky's argument change over time and his thinking on this question develops, the essence of his argument remains basically unchanged [98; 100; 112; 126; 184; 185; 186]. He sees Stalin as the representative of the conservative bureaucracy which has been able to seize control of the revolution and to distort it from its original ends. The bureaucracy has been able to do this chiefly because of the isolation of the revolution, the low level of socio-economic development of Russia and the exhaustion of the proletariat in its struggle to overcome the manifold challenges which confronted it. Exhausted in this way, the proletariat was unable to exercise effective control over the bureaucracy, reflected in the erosion of democracy within party organs, with the result that the bureaucracy was able to consolidate its control. Similar sorts of explanations based upon the growth of the bureaucracy have been popular in some non-Trotskyist sections of the international Marxist movement [22; 181] as well as among some non-Marxist scholars [e.g. 108].

A number of criticisms can be made of Trotsky's line of argument, including its ignoring of other possible sources of Stalinism (see below) and its characterisation of the bureaucracy as conservative when it was under the auspices of this group that the 'revolution from above' was carried out. But the most important criticism for our purposes relates to the linkage drawn between Stalin and the bureaucracy. In his endeavour to play down the role of the individual in history and to emphasise the part played by anonymous social forces, Trotsky portrays Stalin as purely the representative or instrument of bureaucratic social forces. This seems significantly to undervalue the independent role played by Stalin and to denigrate the significant support Stalin received from non-bureaucratic sources. It also creates difficulties in explaining the purges; if the bureaucracy ruled and Stalin was merely its instrument, why did the purges in the second half of the 1930s decimate the bureaucratic structure?

Another type of explanation which gained some currency in the West during the 1950s and 1960s was to see Stalinism as a form of industrialisation [195; 197; 198; 200]. Beginning from the premise that Russia was an underdeveloped country and the Bolsheviks were modernisers aiming to industrialise that country as quickly as possible, this argument declared that the emergence of a dictatorial regime using excessive coercion against the populace was well nigh inevitable. Only if such methods were used could the aim of industrialisation be realised. This line of argument can also be found, in qualified form, in the work of Isaac Deutscher, the former Trotsky supporter and biographer of Stalin [47; 125]. But even if we agree that Bolshevik aims plus the socio-economic conditions in which the new regime found itself made dictatorial coercive rule likely, this is inadequate as an explanation of Stalinism. The only face of Stalinism which it approaches in an explanatory way is the economic, and perhaps by extension the social and cultural; the structuring of political power within the regime cannot be explained by the industrial imperative and Russian backwardness alone.

All of this does not mean that the backwardness of Russia had no part to play in the genesis of Stalinism. However, one cannot use a regime which wished to see significant change within the context of Russian backwardness as sufficient explanation for the emergence of the Stalinist phenomenon. It is important to recognise that in this sort of situation, the political actors involved had a choice of how they would seek to realise their goals. They were not caught up in a deterministic system of values or institutions that had to develop into the Stalinist form. Traditional Russian culture may have fed into the course of Soviet development as some have argued [105; 107; 189; 192], but it did not determine the course of development pursued by the Bolshevik rulers of Russia. Similarly, Bolshevism and Leninism were themselves complex phenomena which had within them the seeds or beginnings of a range of different paths of development; they had no inner essence or logic that automatically led to Stalinism [27; 72 cf. 99; 111; 175]. While the cultural and ideological heritage may have been a factor in helping to shape the decisions made by the political leadership which facilitated the emergence of Stalinism, this heritage was not a determining factor.

If the argument in this book is correct, what was most important for the emergence of Stalinism in all of its faces was the 'revolution from above' at the end of the 1920s–early 1930s and the terror in the late 1930s. The role of these factors brings in considerations both of backwardness and of personal choice on the part of the leaders. No detailed explanation will be offered for the emergence of each of the Stalinist faces; this has to some degree been done elsewhere [106; 67; 50; 73]. Rather the aim is to suggest a link between the Stalinist phenomenon, a particular historical situation, and choices made by the political leadership.

Russian backwardness, particularly in the way it was seen by the leaders of the Bolshevik regime, was an important factor in the 'revolution from above'. This revolution was a revolution against backwardness. The Bolsheviks had come to power in 1917 in the name of socialism, in their view the most advanced stage of human development. But as indicated in Chapter 1, Russian reality sharply contrasted with ideological aspiration. Within the context of international isolation, party leaders searched for a means of breaking this deadlock, of transforming Russian backwardness into the socialist future. It was the means of doing this that the debates of the 1920s explored. When the grain crisis of 1927–8 became apparent, the question of the immediate response to the short-term difficulties merged with that of the longer term strategy of building socialism and resulted in the agricultural collectivisation and forced pace industrialisation of the First Five Year Plan.

Russian backwardness and the desire to escape it was therefore very important in the implementation of the 'revolution from above'. It was also fundamental in the effect that 'revolution from above' had upon the society as a whole. One of the implications of Russian backwardness and of the social and political effects of the October revolution was that the society lacked substantial organisational barriers against the exertion of state power which might limit the effects of such power. The entrepreneurial middle class had been slow to develop in pre-1917 Russia and had therefore not generated that range of institutions and structures which were so important in the defence of middle-class privileges in the West. The anti-bourgeois orientation of the revolution had further weakened such impulses, and although they had made something of a comeback during NEP, as a powerful force they were virtually non-existent. Similarly the working class had been unable to develop strong working-class organisations that could retain their independence from the state, a function both of the assiduity with which the Bolsheviks had worked to control such organisations and the extent of working-class support for the Bolshevik regime. The peasantry remained, for the most part, rooted in their traditional village environment. Although peasant institutions were solidly-based and had shown their capacity to retain significant autonomy vis-à-vis attempts at penetration by party and state organs, they were isolated in the countryside with little wide-scale cooperation between peasant communities. This absence of strong social buffers meant that the exercise of force like that used in the 1929–33 period could ripple through the society with little effective opposition. It also meant that despite the organisational weakness of the political apparatus, it was able to carry through a major transformation of society largely by means of the blunt weapon of coercion [75].

It was the 'revolution from above' which ushered in the Stalinist economic system, stimulated the massive levels of social mobility, and was the means of tying all aspects of cultural production to the political cause. This was achieved because of the inability of the society as a whole and of the individual component sectors of it to generate strong buffers against state action. In this sense, backwardness was important for the emergence of the economic, social and cultural faces of Stalinism.

Backwardness was also important for the emergence of the Stalinist political system. It was the terror of the late 1930s which was instrumental in the consolidation of the political face of Stalinism. This was effectively the turning of the coercive weapon against the political structure, which had largely escaped this during the 'revolution from above'. The role that backwardness played in this was the same as that in 1929–33, the prevention of the emergence of strong institutional barriers to the exercise of personal leadership wielding terror as an instrument of control. The hostile environment facilitated the development of a political system in which the concerns of the moment were more important than stable institution-building, with the result that the political institutions that developed tended to be seen overwhelmingly in an instrumental fashion. Lacking institutional integrity, autonomy and coherence, they could not pose significant barriers against the centralisation of control and the unleashing of the terror [73].

Russian backwardness was therefore a facilitating factor in the emergence of the Stalinist phenomenon, not a determining factor. The backwardness of the society did not ensure that a Stalinist system would emerge, but it did make such a system a possible outcome. What were central to the explanation of Stalinism's genesis were the decisions leading to the 'revolution from above' and the terror. This does not mean that Soviet leaders, in taking decisions about these two events, were consciously deciding thereby to institute what became known as the Stalinist system; in the case of the 'revolution from above', this was clearly far from the thoughts of political actors in 1928–9. Neither does it mean that in either case a single decision ushered in the revolution from above and the terror. In both cases, the events were the result of a string of decisions about which there is still significant uncertainty and debate among scholars. But what is important is that these events were not a natural flow-on of earlier developments; they were sharp breaks resulting from conscious decisions by leading political actors. This means that those arguments that see Stalinism as the inevitable product of the 1917 revolution or of Leninism/Bolshevism are mistaken. Both the revolution and the intellectual corpus of theory which the Bolsheviks carried with them had elements which were consistent with the Stalinist phenomenon (just as they had elements which were totally inconsistent with it). However, it needed the direct intervention on the part of the political actors in introducing the 'revolution from above' and the terror to realise the Stalinist phenomenon in Soviet society.

The importance of political decisions for the emergence of Stalinism raises the question of Stalin's personal responsibility. This has been a frequent theme in writing on the period, both in the West and among sources in the USSR [5; 42; 47; 81; 87; 91; 128; 129; 130; 142; 190; 259]. It has also been the major component in the official Soviet explanation of this phenomenon [96; 219]. The prevalence of this line of argument reflects the fact that our studies of the 1930s were for a considerable time mainly in the form of biographies of Stalin. In its extreme form, the argument for Stalin's personal responsibility posits the existence in Stalin's head of a desire for dictatorial power since at least the early 1920s and his undeviating pursuit of a strategy designed to achieve that goal. Stalin is portrayed as an individual devoid of commitment to ideological goals or principles, adopting policy stances purely for the tactical advantages that would flow from them and thirsting after power regardless of the consequences. Suggestions of mental illness or instability also often appear as Stalin's personality is presented as the main explanatory factor [174; 190]. It is, of course, impossible to plumb the depths of Stalin's psyche and to establish unambiguously the motives which guided his behaviour. It must also be said that an interpretation positing a long-established Stalinist power lust does seem to fit many of the facts as we know them and therefore does offer a possible line of explanation. However, such an interpretation also has some significant weaknesses.

One important line of argument which should stimulate a qualification of the personal responsibility interpretation is that many of the developments which are attributed to the lust for power by Stalin can be explained by other factors. For example, the changes of policy during the 1920s certainly had their factional implications, but their timing was also related to events in the economy (and the international situation) as well; when Stalin's policy changed, there were usually significant developments in these spheres motivating such change. Furthermore, in the cases of those two developments which were so crucial to the emergence of Stalinism, the 'revolution from above' and the terror, other forces in the system clearly favoured both sorts of development. Some in the regional party apparatus, the left wing of the party and many in the central party and state machines favoured the move towards a more directive economic structure and renewed emphasis on heavy industry implicit in the 'revolution from above', even if they were not all convinced of the need for such high levels of coercion or the speed with which results were to be obtained. With regard to the terror, the security apparatus was clearly more than merely a willing instrument, and was a force favouring this sort of development. In short, Stalin was not forcing lines of development on a system in which there was no support for such developments. Rather he was pursuing policy lines for which there was significant support within some sections of the regime. Under such circumstances, the interpretation that Stalin was in part responding to other forces in the system may have as much validity as that which attributes an initiating role solely to the leader.

The personal responsibility argument also assumes a total lack of principle on Stalin's part. It is clear that ambition was a strong part of Stalin's personality, but it does not necessarily follow that all other considerations were thereby missing. It is unlikely that Stalin would have endured the difficulties of life in the pre-1917 socialist underground if he had not been committed to the ideological message of the party. It may be that, once in power, that commitment was overshadowed by considerations of a personal nature, that his drive and ambition became stronger than his attachment to ideological principle. Certainly it is difficult to explain the terror without resort to personal considerations (see below). But we should not assume that Stalin was unchanging. It is more likely that the erosion of the primacy of commitment to ideological values was a more gradual process. If so, it is a matter for debate when that process reached its peak, but the most likely time is in the early 1930s when the battle for collectivisation had been won and the strength of disquiet with Stalin was significant. If this is correct, Stalin was not the unchanging personality driven purely by ambition that the personal responsibility argument often suggests.

Another weakness with the personal responsibility argument is the capacity for controlling events which it seems to attribute to Stalin. Although Stalin had a significant personal political apparatus from an early stage in the life of the Soviet regime [163; 164; 165], the capacity of this organisation to exercise control throughout the system has often been seriously overestimated [73]. The organisational mechanisms through which it functioned at the centre were much more haphazard and slipshod than smoothly efficient, while the tentacles it spread into the localities did not bind local leaders inalienably to the side of the General Secretary. Although Stalin was clearly able to exercise considerable power at the lower levels of the political system, and certainly much more than his opponents, he was not able to build up an extensive, smoothly organised and disciplined political machine that would obey his will. Instead he had to proceed principally through gaining the support of other political leaders at all levels in a coalition-building process. This meant that the degree of control which Stalin was able to exercise prior to the terror was significantly less than many of those who support an unalloyed personal responsibility line of argument would have us believe.

But this does not mean that Stalin bears no personal responsibility at all for the emergence of the system which bears his name. He was clearly in the forefront of both the major changes which were instrumental in the emergence of Stalinism. It was Stalin who introduced the extraordinary measures of grain collection and it was he and his supporters who were central to the increased raising of targets in the collectivisation and industrialisation drives. It was Stalin who was at the forefront of the call for the creation of Soviet technical specialists to replace the bourgeois experts, of the massive increases in party membership, and of the tying of culture to the party's tasks. With regard to the purges, Stalin's responsibility is less reflected in the documents of the period, although some of his speeches clearly did provide a stimulus for the continued search for enemies within the party and society more generally. However, the position he occupied within the regime by the mid-1930s means that the terror could not have unrolled in the face of his opposition. Moreover although he was not aware of the identity of all who were purged, his signature on lists of many to be purged and his arbitrary increasing of the total numbers of those to be arrested noted on documents presented to him [96: *49;* 128: *294*] directly links him with their fate; at the very least his sanction was necessary for the purging of leading members of the party. Furthermore, his position ensured that he could have called a halt to the purges whenever he felt was appropriate, and therefore the fact that they rolled on for as long as they did must be attributed to his direct responsibility.

Stalin was thus clearly personally involved in the two events which were most important in the emergence of Stalinism. He was also of fundamental importance for the continuation of the Stalinist system. The position of personal dictatorship which he occupied meant that he could have structured central politics in any way which he saw fit. The fact that it functioned in the way outlined above means that, at minimum, Stalin was content for it to operate in that way or, more likely, he was positively in favour of such a mode of operation. In this sense, once the system had been established, its maintenance in that form was largely a function of Stalin personally. But like those events which brought Stalinism into being, the continuation of the Stalinist system in the form in which it existed was also supported by other forces in Soviet society. Those who held positions of power and responsibility within all spheres of life under Stalinism had a commitment to the maintenance of that style of doing things. While that commitment may not have been total for all groups, there was nevertheless a reservoir of support for the system among its major components. It was therefore not held in place either by the strength of Stalin's will or the power of the security apparatus alone, but by the strength of support for it throughout the society.

The emergence and development of Stalinism thus cannot be explained on the basis of any one of the three principal lines of explanation suggested above, the contextual, the essentialist or the personalistic. All of these can contribute to that explanation. Clearly Russian backwardness, the authoritarian strands in Bolshevism and Leninism and the personal drive of Stalin all contributed to the emergence of the Stalinist phenomenon. But it is important to recognise also the role of the emergence of a new social structure in the USSR. The Stalinist system, in the form in which it developed, reflects the values and preferences of substantial sections of those moving into positions of authority and privilege in the new system. Most directly, the new economic, social, cultural and political elites had vested interests in the growth of this system because, with its development, their power, positions and prerogatives were consolidated. This represents the emergence of a new value structure in society, a value structure which supported and maintained Stalinism and which had its roots in the newly emerging, urbanised, middle-class aspirant Soviet populace. Here was the social force behind Stalinism which matched the political impetus provided by the 'revolution from above' and the terror. Stalinism constituted the system of the 'new man' in Soviet society.

But while Stalinism was essentially a Soviet phenomenon, historically located in the USSR of the 1930s–50s, the term has had wider application. The Stalinist syndrome outlined in earlier pages was transported into the East European countries that fell under Soviet control after the war, although the continuing dominance of Stalin himself clearly limited the powers the national dictators could exercise. Nevertheless, on Stalin's death, national leaders throughout much of this region sought to sustain the Stalinist model, but with the exception of Albania with only limited success. Stalinism was also extended into the political world outside the borders of states ruled by communist parties. In the international communist movement prior to Khrushchev's denunciation of Stalin in 1956, the term 'Stalinism' referred to adherence to communist orthodoxy, which in practice meant obedience to the line coming from Moscow. After 1956 and the splitting of the communist movement that Khrushchev's destalinisation brought about, 'Stalinism' became a major term of abuse. It had always had such connotations among Trotskyists, but now it became more widespread; it referred to those who supported strict and unthinking centralism, blind obedience to leadership commands, an uncompromising approach to enemies and a tendency to a very expansive view of who constituted an enemy. Unfortunately the currency of the term in its abusive and argumentative form has hindered its utility as a tool of analysis of Soviet development. This is where it belongs and where, devoid of its polemical sheen, it can be of use in expanding our understanding of the Soviet experience.

Conclusion: Dealing with the Legacy of Stalinism

The legacy of the Stalin period was a difficult one for the post-Stalin leadership of the Soviet Union to handle. There were two principal aspects of this, both intimately interconnected but also analytically distinct: how to handle the legacy of Stalin in the public sphere, and what to do about the structural consequences of the Stalinist nature of the Soviet system. Both of these aspects involved major questions for the Soviet system as a whole, and it may be argued that it was the failure to come to grips with them which ultimately was responsible in large part for the fall of the USSR.

[i] The public dimension

This involved discussion of what came to be known as 'the Stalin question'. This phrase encapsulated a whole range of issues, including the reasons for Stalin's rise, how the system came to be established, responsibility for the purges and terror, and the costs of the establishment of the system. However these individual questions were not addressed in an open and forthright manner by Stalin's immediate successors. It would be unrealistic to expect that the post-Stalin elite would openly and unambiguously embrace questioning of all aspects of the system and period which they had recently lived through. It is unrealistic both because of the responsibility that people like Khrushchev, Malenkov, Kaganovich and Voroshilov bore for what happened under Stalin, but also because of the limits to vision possessed by these products of Stalinism. Shaped by their experience of and participation in the Stalinist system, these people could not be expected to be able to offer the deep and wide-ranging critique that was necessary. As a consequence, the first decades after Stalin's death did not witness an open and vigorous discussion and debate about Stalin, Stalinism and its consequences.

However the process of investigation, and of necessity deconstruction, of Stalinism did begin under Khrushchev's leadership in the form of the policy of destalinisation. While the earliest manifestations of this occurred in the policy realm, with some questioning of such Stalinist tenets as the absolute priority of heavy industry and the inevitable opposition of the West, its most striking form came in the so-called 'secret speech' delivered to a closed session of the XX Congress of the party in February 1956 [96]. In this speech, the discussion of the Stalin question was maintained within strict parameters. Khrushchev argued that up until 1934, Stalin had played a positive part in the construction of Soviet socialism, but that after that date his influence had been destructive. In particular, Khrushchev emphasised the way in which Stalin had turned on the party, and was involved in the victimisation of loyal communists. He also argued that Stalin was personally responsible for the setbacks suffered in the early stages of the war, and that he was planning another purge on the eve of his death. The limitations of this sort of approach were clear. Three are important.

(i) By dividing Stalin's role at 1934, Khrushchev was able to argue that the essential aspects of building socialism in the Soviet Union, the revolution, agricultural collectivisation and the First Five Year Plan, were all carried out by the party, while those developments which caused significant damage, principally the purges, were the result of Stalin personally. He was thereby able to absolve the party of responsibility for the hardship and oppression while attributing to it responsibility for the successful construction of the bases of socialism.

(ii) The discussion of hardship and unjustified oppression was restricted only to the party and 'innocent' party members. Khrushchev showed no regret for the loss of life or hardship suffered by non-party members. There was no mention of the famine of 1932–3, no mention of non-party victims of the purges, and no sympathy for the communist losers in the party conflicts of the 1920s; their defeat was justified in the name of the construction of socialism. The victims of Stalin acknowledged by Khrushchev were a very selective group.

(iii) The key to Khrushchev's explanation was what we have earlier labelled the personalist approach. It was the pathological traits and personal idiosyncrasies of the dictator which were responsible for the hardship, abuses and problems of the Stalin years. Khrushchev did acknowledge that the unhealthy atmosphere in the party and lack of restraints on the security apparatus were also important, but these too were at least in part attributable to Stalin himself.

The limitations of Khrushchev's explanation were clear to all; he did not offer a systemic explanation, instead relying on the personal factor. The implication was that with the removal of the vestiges of that personal factor, the irregularities and negative features would be overcome. The removal of Stalinist symbolism was consistent with this: the removal of Stalin's body from the mausoleum on Red Square, the renaming of everything that had been named after Stalin, the removal of his statues and pictures from all places of prominence, and the withdrawal of his written works from public availability, all constitute attempts to remove this personal influence. But this sort of approach could not offer a satisfactory explanation to the Soviet people of the cause of their suffering, nor could it deal satisfactorily with the issue of the genesis of the system.

Khrushchev's effort was clearly politically motivated in two senses. First, it was an attempt to absolve the party of any responsibility for the negative aspects of Soviet rule by placing the blame directly on Stalin personally. It did not ask how the party, whose claims to rule rested on its ability to read the laws of history, had allowed someone like Stalin to achieve control. But Khrushchev's aim of ensuring that discussion of the Stalin legacy did not undermine party legitimacy was clear. Second, Khrushchev sought to use destalinisation to undercut his main political rivals. By associating them closely with Stalin, he sought to discredit them and thereby to strengthen his personal position. This was particularly clear in his speech to the XXI Congress in 1961. These political aims partly explain the limited nature of the Khrushchevian approach.

When Khrushchev had been overthrown, even this limited (albeit significant) approach to the Stalin question was stopped. Under Brezhnev, the public discussion of Stalin in the form it had taken under Khrushchev was closed down, and henceforth public references to the former leader tended to be either neutral in tone or to emphasise his positive aspects. There was no attempt either to mount a sustained critique of the Stalin period or to investigate the systemic roots of the phenomenon. There were even attempts at the time of both the ninetieth and one hundredth anniversaries of his birth to publicly rehabilitate him, but both were aborted. In the official histories, Stalin appeared as a figure with a positive side, while the events of the Stalinist period were treated in a matter-of-fact tone, but without much of the detail. As a result, the scope of the suffering under Stalin did not appear. It was acknowledged that there had been violations of 'Leninist norms' during the Stalin period, but these were seen as minor problems of a basically healthy system. The creation of a new economic structure in the early 1930s, including collectivisation, was seen as both socialist and necessary despite the cost, because it was argued that it was crucial to the survival of the USSR during the war. The interpretation was an anodyne one, which sought to downplay the costs and suffering and emphasise the positive achievements.

However at the same time, the growth of dissident and underground literature provided a ready vehicle for analysis and debate about the Stalin period, its consequences and meaning. The most important dissident studies of Stalinism appeared at this time, including Roy Medvedev's *Let History Judge* [128] and Alexander Solzhenitsyn's *The Gulag Archipelago* [175]. This was also the period that saw the memoirs of people like Mandelshtam [115; 116], Ginzburg [77] and, of a different type, Alliluyeva [3; 4] appear in print. Such volumes, which created quite a stir in the West, circulated within the Soviet intelligentsia in samizdat form, and constituted a ready forum for the continued discussion of questions surrounding this era. But such discussion did not receive any real echo in the official history-writing of the Brezhnev period. For the most part, the official treatment of the Stalin period was sanitised, and although it has been claimed that the Stalinist period was discussed in aesopian terms through the analysis of earlier periods of Russian history, this did not constitute a real debate about Stalinism.

With the opening of the Gorbachev period in 1985, many hoped that this would lead to a revival of public concern with the Stalin question. However official leadership did not at first seem encouraging. In February 1986 Gorbachev referred to Stalinism as 'a concept thought up by enemies of Communism and widely used in order to slander the Soviet Union and socialism as a whole' (*L'Humanité*,

4 February 1986). In his speech on the anniversary of the revolution the following year, Gorbachev quoted approvingly the defeat by 'the Party's leading nucleus headed by Joseph Stalin' of the anti-Leninist opposition during the 1920s and supported the 'great transformation' of the early 1930s, although he did note that during this period the 'administrative command system' took hold throughout socio-political life. More specifically on Stalin, he noted that Stalin was an extremely contradictory personality who made an 'incontestable contribution' to the struggle for socialism but also committed gross political errors and abuses. He said that Stalin was responsible, along with his immediate entourage, for wholesale repressive measures and acts of lawlessness [219]. In this way Gorbachev recognised the problem, but went no further than Khrushchev had done. He did, however, establish a commission to enquire into the repression and to rehabilitate innocent victims, and over succeeding years a large number of people were exonerated of any wrongdoing. These included all former leaders except Trotsky.

However Gorbachev also called for the elimination of all 'blank spots' from Soviet history, and this constituted official sanction for the wave of historical discussion and revelation which came to characterise the Soviet press and the scholarly community. Initial discussion was conducted principally by journalists, but was soon joined by scholarly historians. This discussion ranged widely across all areas of the Stalinist phenomenon. A variety of views emerged regarding the origins of Stalinism, with a particularly popular line being that which attributed primary importance to the link with Lenin. Such a connection discredited and in part helped to delegitimate the whole Soviet system. The costs of the great transformation and possible alternatives (especially that of Bukharin) were canvassed, as were issues of responsibility for and the extent of the famine of 1932–3. The terror, responsibility for it, its extent and whether those involved should be punished, were discussed widely. The Molotov–Ribbentrop Pact, and associated charges that the Soviet Union had brought on the Second World War, the early failings of the Soviet military and responsibility for this, the strengths and weaknesses of Stalin as a military leader, and Soviet responsibility for atrocities committed during the war (e.g. the mass graves at Kuropaty and Katyn) were all debated in a heated fashion. Not one major area of the Stalinist experience remained unexamined, as Soviet writers embarked on this wholescale discussion of the past and process of national soul-searching [213; 216; 240; 242].

For the first time, Soviet citizens were able openly to debate their past and to come to grips with some of the key questions about that past. The problem for the Soviet regime is that as the discussion widened, the threat to regime legitimation increased. As soon as people were able to draw a direct line between Lenin and Stalin, the balancing act that Khrushchev and initially Gorbachev tried to sustain could not be maintained. As the difficulties and horrors of various parts of the Stalin period became evident to all, the attempt to immunise the Soviet system from blame became impossible. Increasingly many associated these difficulties with the system itself, with the result that that system's moral authority was eroded. A significant reason for the lack of popular support for the system at the time of its collapse was this ripping apart of its cloak of legitimacy as a result of the opening up of the Stalin period to popular investigation and discussion.

[ii] The structural consequences of Stalinism

The long-term effects of the four faces of Stalinism contributed significantly to the demise of the Soviet Union, and by seeing the effect each of these faces had on subsequent development, we can gain insights into the dynamics of Soviet decline.

The economic face of Stalinism was particularly important in the ultimate collapse of Soviet power. Three aspects of this were significant. First, the emphasis upon heavy industry and the consequent undervaluing of production in light industry and consumer goods generated the development of a powerful institutional interest within the Soviet economic structure. This interest favoured heavy industry and constituted an important impediment to any attempt to reorder priorities in a major way in the economy. These heavy industrial lobbies were able throughout the post-Stalin period to continue to reinforce the central priority for heavy over light industry, and thereby to consolidate the Stalinist order of priorities, even in the face of attempts to bring about change, such as in the so-called Liberman reforms of 1965.

Second, the extensive nature of the Stalinist economic structure, relying overwhelmingly on increased labour inputs rather than the sort of intensive investment characteristic of industrialised economies meant that when those labour inputs became no longer possible, the structure was not well placed to switch to the needed new form of investment. In this sense, the Soviet economy never grew out of the structure of its initial industrialisation phase. When labour was no longer in ready supply, the system was unable to generate the intensive resources needed to maintain necessary levels of investment and to retool an ageing industrial plant. While not impossible, the generation of such investment would have required the economy to begin to function in a different way to that it had followed in the past, and it was unable to do this.

Third, the effect of these two factors was seen in the chronic short supply of consumer goods in the USSR. As popular expectations rose in the 1960s and 1970s, the economy came under increasing strain. By the middle of the 1970s, the economy was labouring, and this was most evident to Soviet citizens through the drying up of consumer goods supplies. The result was popular disillusionment with the system as it appeared to be failing to keep the promises it made and to satisfy popular expectations.

The effect of this economic failure on popular support for and commitment to the regime was exacerbated by the longer term effects of the cultural face of Stalinism. What was important here was the way in which all cultural production had been tied to the struggle for the achievement of socialism. The deadening effect this had on culture has already been noted. But what increased the effect of this was the vast educational explosion occurring after the war. As the Soviet populace became more highly educated and as, particularly in the 1960s and 1970s, they became more aware of what was happening outside the USSR and especially in the West, the poverty of much Soviet culture became more evident. As the populace became more discerning, satisfaction with their own cultural scene diminished. Soviet readers wanted access to more of what was produced outside, as reflected in the active market for Western books and journals both during Soviet rule and immediately after its fall. Their inability to assuage this hunger deepened their disillusionment.

Similarly the culture stemming from Stalinism may have acted as a straitjacket on creative thinking in the political sphere. There was considerable analysis of questions of importance occurring in the institutes and think tanks across the length and breadth of the Soviet Union, but the capacity to translate some of the results of this into policy terms was severely hampered by the ideological constraints

74

imposed upon the policy agenda. New and innovative ideas had to weather the ideological examination before they could be translated into policy action, and unfortunately much of the thinking which could have been of use in helping to meet the Soviet Union's mounting problems (especially when it involved the question of the introduction of market forces into the economy) did not survive this ideological sieve. In this sense, then, the ideological substratum of culture inhibited the emergence of creative solutions to the Soviet Union's mounting woes.

One result of the social face of Stalinism was also to be important in moulding the course of post-1953 Soviet development. This was the social mobility which occurred in the 1930s and, to a lesser extent, 1940s. This had brought into responsible positions large numbers of people who, through the process of promotion up the hierarchy, had come into the leading positions throughout the system at an early age. As a result of the specific personnel policies pursued by the Brezhnev regime (1964–82), called 'stability of cadres', these people were able substantially to retain their positions until well into the 1980s. By this time they were often very old, with many top leaders in their mid–late seventies while continuing to hold office. The continued domination of the Soviet power structure by this 'Stalinist generation' had significant effects. It meant that during much of the post-Stalin period, the system was being run by people whose formative political experiences lay in the turmoil of the 1920s–1930s and the war. They carried with them values and assumptions which were not necessarily particularly appropriate to the sorts of problems which confronted the Soviet state in the conditions of the 1970s and 1980s. The difference between extensive and intensive development noted above is an example of this. Furthermore it meant that when decisions really needed to be made about reform of the system, those in charge were not only from an era when such problem-solving was not an issue, but were also generally of an age when the sort of flexibility of thinking that was essential was unlikely. The dominance of this group also meant that representatives of new generations, better educated and with different life experiences which could encourage them to be more flexible in their outlook (like Gorbachev) were prevented from reaching positions of power in the 1960s and 1970s. In this sense, the continuing dominance of the Stalin generation acted as a stultifying force on Soviet development.

This was also related to the political face of Stalinism. The essential feature of the political face was personal dictatorship. The system had been created to respond to the imperatives of the leader, and when that leader disappeared, problems resulted. These were not only the immediate problems of succession, but the longer term (and at the time largely unrecognised) problems of system functioning. If the system had been set up as a series of overlapping and competing bureaucratic structures, it required intervention from above to maintain the balance and to prevent it from locking itself into immobility and bureaucratic conflict. Khrushchev's leadership was an attempt to sustain an interventionist style of leadership without the threat of terror to back it up. It failed, because of the way in which Khrushchev alienated all of the powerful interests and yet had no effective weapon with which to overcome their opposition. In partial reaction to this, Brezhnev chose a leadership style that was non-interventionist. He chose to leave lower level political officials in place virtually regardless of how they performed, with the result that the sorts of informal cliques of power at all levels of the political structure which had been so commented upon in the 1930s once again became prominent. Indeed, the centre took such a hands-off approach, that the structure became effectively balkanised. When Gorbachev came to power, he too sought to play an active, interventionist role in order to bring about major change in the system, but ultimately he too failed. By eschewing terror like Khrushchev, he too needed a weapon with which to combat his opponents. He turned to openness and democratisation, relying on the rank-and-file party members and the mass of the population both to place pressure upon his opponents and to press the reforms forward. However the system he inherited proved not to be sufficiently flexible to be able to accommodate the entry of such forces and the restructuring that this would have involved. This history seems to suggest that, given the structure inherited from Stalin, a single leader was unlikely to be able to force through major measures in the absence of the threat of substantial coercion.

The other aspect of the political face of Stalinism which is relevant here is the interlocking nature of all parts of the Soviet system. The effect of this was that no single part of the system could be isolated from major changes in any other part. Effective economic reform could not be conducted without political change; increased openness could not be introduced without democratisation;

political reform could not be introduced without economic restructuring. This means that, ultimately, significant reform, at least in a decentralising direction, was impossible unless it was to be a root and branch restructuring of Soviet fundamentals. This would have involved a reworking of the legacies of the four faces of Stalinism. But given the immensity of this task and the circumstances prevailing at the time, this was a job that lay beyond the capacities of the Soviet leadership that took the reins in 1985.

None of this was inevitable. Had reformist measures been introduced earlier when the economic pressures were not so intense and when popular disillusionment had not been as deep, it may be that substantial reform would have been possible and these connections could have been overcome. But as it was, with the effort at major reform left until the late-1980s, the Stalinist legacy was too powerful to overcome.

With a new political system in place in Russia, the Stalin question has again dropped off the public agenda. Although there are minimal restrictions on publication and archival access has been greatly improved, this has not led to intense public or scholarly debate in Russia on 'the Stalin question'. Contemporary issues and problems have pushed many historical perspectives from view. But even so, if we are to understand the Russian present, we must take account of the Soviet legacy, and this must involve coming to grips with the issue of Stalinism. Thus Stalinism remains relevant not only as a focus of historical analysis, but as a confining condition of future post-Soviet development.

Select Bibliography

[1] G. F. Alexandrov *et al.*, *Joseph Stalin. A Short Biography* (Moscow, 1947). An official biography.

[2] Tariq Ali, *The Stalinist Legacy. Its Impact on 20th Century World Politics* (Harmondsworth, 1984). Selection of articles from and about the Trotskyist perspective.

[3] Svetlana Alliluyeva, *Twenty Letters to a Friend* (Harmondsworth, 1968). Memoirs of Stalin's daughter.

[4] Svetlana Alliluyeva, *Only One Year* (New York, 1969). Second volume of memoirs of Stalin's daughter.

[5] Anton Antonov-Ovseyenko, *The Time of Stalin. Portrait of a Tyranny* (New York, 1981). Sensationalist account by the son of one of Stalin's victims.

[6] John A. Armstrong, *The Politics of Totalitarianism. The Communist Party of the Soviet Union From 1934 to the Present* (New York, 1961). A major study of the last two decades of Stalin's rule.

[7] Abdurahman Avtorkhanov, *Stalin and the Soviet Communist Power. A Study in the Technology of Power* (New York, 1959). A study of party development by a former party official. But see [208].

[8] Siegfried Bahne, 'Trotsky on Stalin's Russia', *Survey*, 41 (1962).

[9] Kendall E. Bailes, *Technology and Society under Lenin and Stalin. Origins of the Soviet Technical Intelligentsia, 1917–1941* (Princeton, 1978). An important study of the role and fate of the technical intelligentsia.

[10] John Barber, *Soviet Historians in Crisis 1928–1932* (London, 1981). Study of the fate of the history profession in the cultural revolution.

[11] John Barber, 'Stalin's Letter to the Editors of Proletarskaya Revoliutsiya', *Soviet Studies*, XXXVIII, 1 (1976). Useful study of Stalin's intervention in historical affairs.

[12] Henri Barbusse, *Stalin. A New World Seen Through One Man* (London, 1935). An enthusiastic biography, serialised in *Pravda*.

[13] Frederick Barghoorn, 'Stalinism and the Russian Cultural Heritage', *Problems of Communism*, II, 1 (1953).

[14] Charles Bettelheim, *Class Struggles in the USSR First Period: 1917–1923* (Hassocks, 1977). An important Marxist attempt to explain the course of Soviet development.

[15] Charles Bettelheim, *Class Struggles in the USSR Second Period: 1923–1930* (Hassocks, 1978).

[16] Seweryn Bialer, *Stalin and His Generals* (New York, 1969). Stalin's

relationship with his army commanders through the memoirs of the latter.

[17] Seweryn Bialer, *Stalin's Successors. Leadership, stability and change in the Soviet Union* (Cambridge, 1980). An important study of the Stalinist system and its legacy.

[18] Daniel R. Brower, 'Collectivized Agriculture in Smolensk: The Party, the Peasantry, and the Crisis of 1932', *The Russian Review*, 36, 2 (1977).

[19] Georg Brunner, 'The essence of Stalinism', *Problems of Communism*, XXX, 3 (1981).

[20] Wlodzimierz Brus, 'Stalinism and the "People's Democracies"', Robert C. Tucker (ed.), *Stalinism. Essays in Historical Interpretation* (New York, 1977).

[21] M. M. Bullitt, 'Towards a Marxist Theory of Aesthetics: the Development of Socialist Realism in the Soviet Union', *The Russian Review*, XXXV, 1 (1976).

[22] Pavel Campeanu, *The Origins of Stalinism. From Leninist Revolution to Stalinist Society* (Armonk, 1986). An important study that sees Stalinism resulting from the contradictory nature of the Russian revolution.

[23] E. H. Carr, *A History of Soviet Russia* (Harmondsworth, 1966–76). Classic multi-volume history.

[24] E. H. Carr, *The Russian Revolution From Lenin to Stalin 1917–1929* (London, 1979). Single volume summary of [23].

[25] Helene Carrere D'Encausse, *Stalin. Order Through Terror* (London, 1981). Excellent history of the Stalin period.

[26] Katerina Clark, 'Utopian Anthropology as a Context for Stalinist Literature', in Robert C. Tucker (ed.), *Stalinism. Essays in Historical Interpretation* (New York, 1977). Stimulating study of literary development.

[27] Stephen F. Cohen, 'Bolshevism and Stalinism', in Robert C. Tucker (ed.), *Stalinism. Essays in Historical Interpretation* (New York, 1977). Stimulating discussion of the continuity thesis.

[28] Stephen F. Cohen, *Bukharin and the Bolshevik Revolution. A Political Biography, 1888–1938* (New York, 1973). Superb biography of Bukharin.

[29] Stephen F. Cohen, 'Stalin's Terror as Social History', *The Russian Review*, 45, 4 (1986). Critique of social historians.

[30] S. Cohen, 'Stalin's revolution reconsidered', *Slavic Review*, XXXII, 2 (1973).

[31] Lucio Colletti, 'The Question of Stalin', *New Left Review*, 61 (1970). A Trotskyist study.

[32] Robert Conquest, *The Great Terror* (Harmondsworth, 1971). The standard study of the purges.

[33] Robert Conquest, *'The Great Terror* Revised', *Survey*, 16, 1 (1971).

[34] Robert Conquest, *The Harvest of Sorrow. Soviet collectivization and the terror famine* (London, 1986). Major study of famine of 1932–3.

[35] Robert Conquest, *Inside Stalin's Secret Police. NKVD Politics 1936–39* (Stanford, 1985). Focuses purely upon personnel movements.

[36] Robert Conquest, *The Nation Killers: the Soviet Deportation of Nationalities* (London, 1970).

[37] Alexander Dallin, 'Allied Leadership in the Second World War: Stalin', *Survey*, 21, 1/2 (Winter–Spring 1975).

[38] Robert Vincent Daniels, *The Conscience of the Revolution. Communist Opposition in Soviet Russia* (New York, 1969). Best study of factional conflict of 1920s.

[39] Robert V. Daniels, *The Stalin Revolution. Foundations of Soviet Totalitarianism* (Lexington, 1965). Useful collection of articles.

[40] Robert V. Daniels, 'Stalin's Rise to Dictatorship, 1922–29', Alexander Dallin and Alan F. Westin (eds), *Politics in the Soviet Union. 7 Cases* (New York, 1966). Useful summary account.

[41] R. W. Davies, *The Industrialisation of Soviet Russia. 1. The Socialist Offensive. The Collectivisation of Soviet Agriculture, 1929–1930* (London, 1980). First volume of a multi-volume series, continuing the work of Carr. See R. W. Davies [210; 211] below.

[42] Alex De Jonge, *Stalin and the Shaping of the Soviet Union* (London, 1986). Popularly-written biography.

[43] Edmund Demaitre, 'Stalin and the Era of "Rational Irrationality"', *Problems of Communism*, XVI, 6 (1967).

[44] Isaac Deutscher, *The Prophet Armed Trotsky: 1879–1921* (Oxford, 1954). First volume of the classic biography; also [45] and [46].

[45] Isaac Deutscher, *The Prophet Unarmed Trotsky: 1921–1929* (Oxford, 1959).

[46] Isaac Deutscher, *The Prophet Outcast Trotsky: 1929–1940* (Oxford, 1963).

[47] Isaac Deutscher, *Stalin. A Political Biography* (Harmondsworth, 1966). Excellent biography.

[48] Milovan Djilas, *Conversations with Stalin* (Harmondsworth, 1969). Memoirs of Stalin in the post-war period.

[49] M. R. Dohan, 'The Economic Origins of Soviet Autarky 1927/28–1934', *Slavic Review*, XXXV, 4 (1976).

[50] Vera J. Dunham, *In Stalin's Time: middle class values in Soviet fiction* (Cambridge, 1979). An excellent study of the course of literary development.

[51] Timothy Dunmore, *Soviet Politics 1945–53* (London, 1984). Focuses mainly on individual policy sectors.

[52] Timothy Dunmore, *The Stalinist Command Economy. The Soviet State Apparatus and Economic Policy 1945–53* (London, 1980). Economic structure and policy in the post-war period.

[53] Geoff Eley, 'History With the Politics Left Out – Again?', *The Russian Review*, 45, 4 (1986). Critique of social historians.

[54] Jean Elleinstein, *The Stalin Phenomenon* (London, 1976). A Trotskyist analysis.

[55] Alexander Erlich, 'Stalinism and Marxian Growth Models', in Robert C. Tucker (ed.), *Stalinism. Essays in Historical Interpretation* (New York, 1977).

[56] Alexander Erlich, 'Stalin's Views on Soviet Economic Development',

in E. J. Simmons (ed.), *Continuity and Change in Russian and Soviet Thought* (New York, 1955).

[57] Merle Fainsod, *Smolensk Under Soviet Rule* (New York, 1958). Study of the Smolensk archives.

[58] Sheila Fitzpatrick, 'Afterward: Revisionism revisited', *The Russian Review*, 45, 4 (1986). Defence of social history approach.

[59] Sheila Fitzpatrick (ed.), *Cultural Revolution in Russia, 1928–1931* (Bloomington, 1978). Excellent collection of articles on the cultural revolution period.

[60] Sheila Fitzpatrick, 'Culture and Politics Under Stalin: A Reappraisal, *Slavic Review*, 35, 2 (1976). Shows how control in the cultural field rested on the role played by cultural figures as models.

[61] Sheila Fitzpatrick, *Education and Social Mobility in the Soviet Union 1921–1934* (Cambridge, 1979). Study of the relationship between education and social mobility.

[62] Sheila Fitzpatrick, 'The Emergence of Glaviskusstvo: class war on the cultural front: Moscow 1928–29', *Soviet Studies*, XXIII, 2 (1971).

[63] Sheila Fitzpatrick, 'The Foreign Threat during the First Five-Year Plan', *Soviet Union*, 5, 1 (1978).

[64] Sheila Fitzpatrick, 'New Perspectives on Stalinism', *The Russian Review*, 45, 4 (1986). Defends the social history approach.

[65] Sheila Fitzpatrick, *The Russian Revolution* (Oxford, 1982). Stimulating social history of the revolution, 1900-mid 1930s.

[66] Sheila Fitzpatrick, 'The Russian Revolution and Social Mobility: A Re-examination of the Question of Social Support for the Soviet Regime in the 1920s and 1930s', *Politics and Society*, 13, 2 (1984). Stimulating discussion of the link between social support and mobility.

[67] Sheila Fitzpatrick, 'Stalin and the Making of a New Elite, 1928–1939', *Slavic Review*, 38, 3 (1979). Discusses the connection between the terror and social mobility.

[68] Bruce Franklin (ed.), *The Essential Stalin. Major Theoretical Writings 1905–52* (London, 1973). Some of Stalin's writings reprinted, with an enthusiastic introduction.

[69] Valentino Gerratana, 'Stalin, Lenin and "Leninism"', *New Left Review*, 103 (May–June 1977). Discusses the relationship between the Lenin and Stalin periods.

[70] J. Arch Getty, *Origins of the Great Purges. The Soviet Communist Party Reconsidered, 1933–1938* (Cambridge, 1985). Revisionist history of the party in the 1930s.

[71] J. Arch Getty, 'Party and Purge in Smolensk: 1933–1937', *Slavic Review*, 42, 1 (1983). Also the following comments by Tucker and Rosenfeldt. Revisionist study of the origins of the purges.

[72] Graeme Gill, 'Bolshevism and the Party Form', *Australian Journal of Politics and History*, 34, 1 (1988). Study of the diversity within Bolshevism.

[73] Graeme Gill, *The Origins of the Stalinist Political System* (Cambridge, 1990). Study of the development of the structural bases of the Stalinist political system.

[74] Graeme Gill, 'Political Myth and Stalin's Quest for Authority in the Party', in T. H. Rigby, Archie Brown and Peter Reddaway (eds), *Authority, Power and Policy in the USSR. Essays dedicated to Leonard Schapiro* (London, 1980). Study of Stalin's manipulation of regime symbolism in an attempt to consolidate his position.

[75] Graeme Gill, 'The Single Party as an Agent of Development: Lessons from the Soviet Experience', *World Politics*, XXXIX, 4 (July 1987). Argues for the weakness of the party organisation at the time of collectivisation.

[76] Graeme Gill, 'Stalinism and Institutionalization: The Nature of Stalin's Regional Support', in John W. Strong (ed.), *Essays on Revolutionary Culture and Stalinism* (Columbus, 1989). Studies the changing nature of Stalin's regional support.

[77] Evgenia S. Ginzburg, *Into the Whirlwind* (Harmondsworth, 1968). Major memoir of purge period.

[78] Zaga Golubovic, 'The History of Russia Under Stalin', *New Left Review*, 104 (July–August 1977). Review of Medvedev [128].

[79] Alvin W. Gouldner, 'Stalinism: A Study of Internal Colonialism', *Telos*, 34 (1977–78).

[80] A. James Gregor, 'Fascism and Modernization: Some Addenda', *World Politics*, XXVI, 3 (April 1974).

[81] Ian Grey, *Stalin. Man of History* (London, 1979). A popular biography.

[82] Werner G. Hahn, *Postwar Soviet Politics. The Fall of Zhdanov and the Defeat of Moderation, 1946–53* (Ithaca, 1982). A major study of the post-war period, and particularly the place in it of Zhdanov.

[83] Neil Harding, *Lenin's Political Thought* (London, 1977 and 1981), 2 vols. The major study of Lenin's thought.

[84] J. Harris, 'Historians on Stalin', *Soviet Union*, 1, 1 (1974).

[85] Jonathan Harris, 'The Origins of the Conflict Between Malenkov and Zhdanov: 1939–1941', *Slavic Review*, 35, 2 (1976).

[86] Mark Harrison, *Soviet Planning in Peace and War 1938–1945* (Cambridge, 1985). Study of wartime planning process.

[87] Ronald Hingley, *Joseph Stalin: Man and Legend* (London, 1974). Useful biography.

[88] *History of the Communist Party of the Soviet Union (Bolsheviks). Short Course* (Moscow, 1939). Official history, reputedly written in part by Stalin.

[89] Holland Hunter, 'The overambitious First Soviet Five Year Plan', *Slavic Review*, XXXII, 2 (1973).

[90] Eugene Huskey, *Russian Lawyers and the Soviet State. The Origin and Development of the Soviet Bar, 1917–1931* (Princeton, 1986). Study of the development of the Soviet bar.

[91] H. Montgomery Hyde, *Stalin. The History of a Dictator* (London, 1971). Popular biography.

[92] David Joravsky, *The Lysenko Affair* (Cambridge, Mass, 1970).

[93] A. Kemp-Welch, 'Stalinism and Intellectual Order', in T. H. Rigby, Archie Brown and Peter Reddaway (eds), *Authority, Power and Policy in the USSR. Essays dedicated to Leonard Schapiro* (London, 1980). A study of decision-making in the intellectual sphere.

[94] Peter Kenez, 'Stalinism as Humdrum Politics', *The Russian Review*, 45, 4 (1986). Critique of social history approach.

[95] G. Kern, 'Solzhenitsyn's Portrait of Stalin', *Slavic Review,* XXXIII, 1 (1974).

[96] N. S. Khrushchev, 'On the Cult of Personality and its Consequences', in T. H. Rigby (ed.), *The Stalin Dictatorship* (Sydney, 1968). Khrushchev's famous secret speech on the Stalin question.

[97] *Khrushchev Remembers* (ed. Strobe Talbot), (London, 1971, 1974), 2 vols. Khrushchev's memoirs.

[98] Baruch Knei-Paz, *The Social and Political Thought of Leon Trotsky* (Oxford, 1978). The most complete study of Trotsky's thought.

[99] Leszek Kolakowski, 'Marxist Roots of Stalinism', in Robert C. Tucker (ed.), *Stalinism. Essays in Historical Interpretation* (New York, 1977). Argues for a direct link between Marxism and Stalinism.

[100] Martin Krygier, '"Bureaucracy" in Trotsky's Analysis of Stalinism', in Marian Sawer (ed.), *Socialism and the New Class: Towards the Analysis of Structural Inequality within Socialist Societies* (APSA Monograph No. 19, Bedford Park, 1978).

[101] Nicholas Lampert, *The Technical Intelligentsia and the Soviet State. A Study of Soviet Managers and Technicians 1928–1935* (London, 1979). Useful study of the technical intelligentsia.

[102] David Lane, *Leninism: A Sociological Interpretation* (Cambridge, 1981).

[103] Nathan Leites, Elsa Bernaut and Raymond L. Garthoff, 'Politburo Images of Stalin', *World Politics*, III, 3 (April 1951).

[104] Moshe Lewin, *Lenin's Last Struggle* (New York, 1968). An important study of the late (1921–4) Lenin.

[105] Moshe Lewin, *The Making of the Soviet System. Essays in the Social History of Interwar Russia* (New York, 1985). Stimulating collection of essays.

[106] Moshe Lewin, *Russian Peasants and Soviet Power. A Study of Collectivization* (London, 1968). Detailed study of early collectivisation.

[107] Moshe Lewin, 'The Social Background of Stalinism', in Robert C. Tucker (ed.), *Stalinism. Essays in Historical Interpretation* (New York, 1977). Stimulating essay on the first five year plan period and its implications.

[108] Moshe Lewin, 'Society and the Stalinist state in the period of the Five Year Plans', *Social History*, 1 (1976). Thought-provoking social history.

[109] Marcel Liebman, *Leninism Under Lenin* (London, 1975). Useful study of Lenin's thought and practice.

[110] D.A. Loeber, 'Bureaucracy in a Workers' State: E. B. Pashukanis and the Struggle Against Bureaucratism in the Soviet Union' *Soviet Union*, VI, 2 (1979).

[111] David W. Lovell, *From Marx to Lenin. An Evaluation of Marx's Responsibility for Soviet Authoritarianism* (Cambridge, 1984).

[112] David W. Lovell, *Trotsky's Analysis of Soviet Bureaucratization* (London, 1985).

[113] Georg Lukács, 'Reflections on the Cult of Stalin', *Survey*, 47 (April 1963).

[114] R. A. Maguire, *Red Virgin Soil: Soviet Literature in the 1920s* (Princeton, 1968).

[115] Nadezhda Mandelstam, *Hope Abandoned* (London, 1974). Memoirs of a purge victim. Also [116].

[116] Nadezhda Mandelstam, *Hope Against Hope* (London, 1971).

[117] Roberta T. Manning, *Government in the Soviet Countryside in the Stalinist Thirties. The Case of Belyi Raion in 1937* (The Carl Beck Papers in Russian and East European Studies, Paper No. 301, Pittsburgh, 1984). Study showing the weakness of party control in the countryside.

[118] Roberta Manning, 'Peasants and the Party: Rural Administration in the Soviet Countryside on the Eve of World War II', in John W. Strong (ed.), *Essays on Revolutionary Culture and Stalinism* (Columbus, 1989). As for [117].

[119] Mihailo Markovic, 'Stalinism and Marxism', in Robert C. Tucker (ed.), *Stalinism. Essays in Historical Interpretation* (New York, 1977). Argues that Marxism did not lead to Stalinism.

[120] William O. McCagg, Jr, *Stalin Embattled 1943–1948* (Detroit, 1978). Controversial study emphasising limits of Stalin's power.

[121] Martin McCauley, *Stalin and Stalinism* (Harlow, 1983). Mainly descriptive account of Stalin period.

[122] Robert H. McNeal, 'The Decisions of the CPSU and the Great Purge', *Soviet Studies*, XXIII, 2 (1971). Important study of party decisions relating to the purges.

[123] Robert H. McNeal (ed.), *Resolutions and Decisions of the Communist Party of the Soviet Union* (Toronto, 1974). Important multi-volume set of party decisions.

[124] Robert H. McNeal, *Stalin's Works. An Annotated Bibliography* (Stanford, 1967).

[125] Robert H. McNeal, 'Trotskyist Interpretations of Stalinism', in Robert C. Tucker (ed.), *Stalinism. Essays in Historical Interpretation* (New York, 1977). Focuses on changes in interpretation of Stalinism by the Trotskyist school.

[126] Robert H. McNeal, 'Trotsky's Interpretation of Stalin', in T. H. Rigby (ed.), *Stalin* (Englewood Cliffs, 1966). Focuses on Trotsky's view.

[127] Roy Medvedev, *All Stalin's Men* (Oxford, 1983). Study of Stalin's colleagues.

[128] Roy Medvedev, *Let History Judge. The Origins and Consequences of Stalinism* (London, 1971). Landmark study by Soviet dissident.

[129] Roy A. Medvedev, 'New Pages from the Political Biography of Stalin', in Robert C. Tucker (ed.), *Stalinism. Essays in Historical Interpretation* (New York, 1977). Addendum to [128].

[130] Roy A. Medvedev, *On Stalin and Stalinism* (Oxford, 1979). Addendum to [128].

[131] Zhores A. Medvedev, *The Rise and Fall of T. D. Lysenko* (New York, 1969). Study by Soviet dissident of notorious Lysenko affair.

[132] Alfred G. Meyer, 'Coming to Terms with the Past ... And With One's Older Colleagues', *The Russian Review*, 45, 4 (1986). Comment on approach of the social historians.

[133] Alfred G. Meyer, *Leninism* (New York, 1957). Standard study of Leninism.

[134] Alfred G. Meyer, 'The War Scare of 1927', *Soviet Union, 5, 1* (1978).

[135] Ralph Miliband, 'Stalin and After. Some Comments on Two Books by Roy Medvedev', *The Socialist Register* (1973).

[136] James R. Millar and Alec Nove, 'A Debate on Collectivization. Was Stalin Really Necessary?', *Problems of Communism*, XXV, 4 (1976). Important discussion of motivations behind collectivisation.

[137] A. Nekrich, *The Punished Peoples: the Deportation and Tragic Fate of Soviet Minorities at the End of the Second World War* (New York, 1978). Study by Soviet historian.

[138] Boris I. Nicolaevsky, *Power and the Soviet Elite* (Ann Arbor, 1965). Includes the famous Letter of an Old Bolshevik based on Nicolaevsky's discussions with Bukharin.

[139] Alec Nove, *An Economic History of the USSR* (Harmondsworth, 1972). An excellent study of Soviet economic development.

[140] Alec Nove, *Stalinism and After* (London, 1975). Stimulating popular study.

[141] Alec Nove, 'Was Stalin Really Necessary?', in Alec Nove, *Economic Rationality and Soviet Politics or Was Stalin Really Necessary?* (New York, 1964). Classic argument regarding collectivisation.

[142] Robert Payne, *The Rise and Fall of Stalin* (London, 1966). Popular biography.

[143] 'The Personality Cult', *Survey*, 63 (April 1967). Transcript of discussion by Soviet historians.

[144] Roger Pethybridge, *The Social Prelude to Stalinism* (London, 1974). Stimulating discussion of relationship between Stalinism and backwardness.

[145] J. Quigley, 'The 1926 Soviet Family Code: Retreat from Free Love', *Soviet Union*, 6, 2 (1979).

[146] Gavriel D. Ra'anan, *International Policy Formation in the USSR. Factional 'Debates' during the Zhdanovshchina* (Hamden, 1983). Major study of factional politics in the post-war USSR.

[147] Christian Rakovsky, *Selected Writings on Opposition in the USSR 1923–30* (London, 1980). Writings by a prominent oppositionist.

[148] Michal Reiman, *The Birth of Stalinism. The USSR on the Eve of the 'Second Revolution'* (Bloomington, 1987). An important study of the crisis at the end of the 1920s.

[149] Michal Reiman, 'Political Trials of the Stalinist Era', *Telos*, 54 (1982–3).

[150] Michal Reiman, 'The Russian Revolution and Stalinism: A Political Problem and its Historiographic Content', in John W. Strong (ed.), *Essays on Revolutionary Culture and Stalinism* (Columbus, 1989).

[151] *Report of Court Proceedings in the Case of the Anti-Soviet 'Bloc of Rights and Trotskyites'* (Moscow, 1938). Official court proceedings of the purge trials. Also [152] and [153].

[152] *Report of Court Proceedings in the Case of the Anti-Soviet Trotskyite Centre* (Moscow, 1937).

[153] *Report of Court Proceedings in the Case of Trotskyite–Zinovievite Terrorist Centre* (Moscow, 1936).

[154] T. H. Rigby, *Communist Party Membership in the USSR 1917–1967* (Princeton, 1968). Standard study of party membership.

[155] T. H. Rigby, 'Early Provincial Cliques and the Rise of Stalin', *Soviet Studies*, XXXIII, 1 (January 1981). Study of the beginnings of personnel manipulation.

[156] T. H. Rigby (ed.), *Stalin* (Englewood Cliffs, 1966). Useful collection of papers on Stalin.

[157] T. H. Rigby, 'Stalinism and the Mono-Organisational Society', in Robert C. Tucker (ed.), *Stalinism. Essays in Historical Interpretation* (New York, 1977). Stimulating interpretation of the nature of Stalinism.

[158] T. H. Rigby, 'Was Stalin a Disloyal Patron?', *Soviet Studies*, XXXVIII, 3 (July 1986). Useful qualification to the general view about the victims of the purges.

[159] Gabor Rittersporn, 'The 1930s in the Longue Durée of Soviet History', *Telos*, 53 (1982).

[160] Gabor Tamas Rittersporn, 'Soviet Officialdom and Political Evolution. Judiciary Apparatus and Penal Policy in the 1930s', *Theory and Society*, 13 (1984). An interesting study of law and its application during the 1930s.

[161] Gabor Tamas Rittersporn, 'Soviet Politics in the 1930s: Rehabilitating Society', *Studies in Comparative Communism*, XIX, 2 (Summer 1986). Stimulating study of the position and problems of lower-level officials.

[162] William G. Rosenberg, 'Smolensk in the 1920s: Party-Worker Relations and the "Vanguard" Problem', *The Russian Review*, 36, 2 (1977).

[163] Niels Erik Rosenfeldt, '"The Consistory of the Communist Church": The Origins and Development of Stalin's Secret Chancellery', *Russian History*, 9, 2–3 (1982). Further development of (164).

[164] Niels Erik Rosenfeldt, *Knowledge and Power. The Role of Stalin's Secret Chancellery in the Soviet System of Government* (Copenhagen, 1978). An important study of Stalin's personal apparatus.

[165] Niels Erik Rosenfeldt, 'Stalinism as a System of Communication', in John W. Strong (ed.), *Essays on Revolutionary Culture and Stalinism* (Columbus, 1989). Shows the importance of Stalin's personal apparatus.

[166] Leonard Schapiro, *The Communist Party of the Soviet Union* (London, 1970). The classic history of the party.

[167] Leonard Schapiro, *The Origin of the Communist Autocracy. Political Opposition in the Soviet State: First Phase, 1917–1922* (New York, 1965). Path-breaking study of early opposition.

[168] Victor Serge, *From Lenin to Stalin* (New York, 1973).

[169] Robert Service, *The Russian Revolution 1900–1927* (London, 1986 & 1991). Excellent discussion of many of the main questions relating to this period.

[170] Robert Sharlet, 'Stalinism and Soviet Legal Culture', in Robert C. Tucker (ed.), *Stalinism. Essays in Historical Interpretation* (New York, 1977). Stimulating discussion of the place of law.

[171] Marshall Shatz, *Stalin, the Great Purge, and Russian History. A New Look at the 'New Class'* (The Carl Beck Papers in Russian and East European Studies, Paper No. 305, Pittsburgh, 1984).

[172] L. Shelley, 'Soviet Criminology: The Birth and Demise 1917–1936', *Slavic Review*, XXXVIII, 4 (1979).

[173] H. Gordon Skilling, 'Stalinism and Czechoslovak Political Culture', in Robert C. Tucker (ed.), *Stalinism. Essays in Historical Interpretation* (New York, 1977).

[174] Alexander Solzhenitsyn, *The First Circle* (London, 1968). Includes an important psychological portrait of Stalin by the leading dissident writer.

[175] Alexander Solzhenitsyn, *The Gulag Archipelago* (Glasgow, 1973–8). An important study of terror by one of its leading victims.

[176] Boris Souvarine, *Stalin: a critical survey of Bolshevism* (New York, 1939). A valuable early biography.

[177] J. V. Stalin, *Works* (Moscow, 1953–5), vols 1–13.

[178] John W. Strong (ed.), *Essays on Revolutionary Culture and Stalinism* (Columbus, 1989). An interesting collection of articles on a variety of themes.

[179] T. Szamuely, 'The Elimination of Opposition Between the Sixteenth and Seventeenth Congresses of the CPSU', *Soviet Studies*, XVII, 3 (1966).

[180] R. Taagepera, 'Soviet collectivization of Estonian agriculture: The deportation phase', *Soviet Studies*, XXXII, 3 (1980).

[181] Palmiro Togliatti, '9 Domande sullo Stalinismo', *Nuovi Argomenti*, No. 20 (16 June 1956), reprinted in *The Anti-Stalin Campaign and International Communism. A Selection of Documents* (New York, 1956). An important early European communist response to Khrushchev's secret speech [96].

[182] Leon Trotsky, *The Challenge of the Left Opposition (1923–25)* (New York, 1975).

[183] Leon Trotsky, *My Life* (New York, 1970).

[184] Leon Trotsky, *The New Course* (Ann Arbor, 1965).

[185] Leon Trotsky, *The Permanent Revolution and Results and Prospects* (New York, 1970).

[186] Leon Trotsky, *The Revolution Betrayed* (New York, 1970). The most complete statement of Trotsky's explanation for the emergence of Stalinism. The other references show the development of his thought.

[187] Leon Trotsky, *Stalin. An Appraisal of the Man and His Influence* (London, 1947).

[188] Robert C. Tucker, 'The Rise of Stalin's Personality Cult', *American Historical Review*, 84, 2 (April 1979). Useful study of the origins of the cult.

[189] Robert C. Tucker, *The Soviet Political Mind. Studies in Stalinism and Post-Stalin Change* (New York, 1971).

[190] Robert C. Tucker, *Stalin as Revolutionary 1879–1929. A Study in History and Personality* (London, 1973). A psycho-history biography.

[191] Robert C. Tucker (ed.), *Stalinism. Essays in Historical Interpretation* (New York, 1977). A stimulating set of interpretative essays.

[192] Robert C. Tucker, 'Stalinism as Revolution from Above', and 'Some Questions on the Scholarly Agenda', in [191]. Thoughtful contributions to the volume.

[193] Robert C. Tucker, 'Svetlana Alliluyeva as witness of Stalin', *Slavic Review*, XXVII, 2 (1968).

[194] Adam B. Ulam, *Stalin. The Man and His Era* (London, 1973). A good biography.

[195] Adam B. Ulam, *The Unfinished Revolution. An Essay on the Sources of Influence of Marxism and Communism* (Vintage, 1960). An interesting discussion of the nature of Marxism.

[196] G. R. Urban, *Stalinism. Its Impact on Russia and the World* (Aldershot, 1982). A useful set of essays.

[197] Theodore H. Von Laue, 'Stalin among the Moral and Political Imperatives, or How to Judge Stalin', *Soviet Union*, 8, 1 (1981). A controversial evaluation of Stalin.

[198] Theodore H. Von Laue, 'Stalin in Focus', *Slavic Review*, 42, 3 (1983). Controversial evaluation.

[199] Theodore H. Von Laue, 'Stalin reviewed', *Soviet Union*, 11, 1 (1984).

[200] Theodore H. Von Laue, *Why Lenin? Why Stalin? A Reappraisal of the Russian Revolution, 1900–1930* (Philadelphia, 1964). On the importance of industrialisation in the history of the revolution.

[201] Bertram D. Wolfe, *Three Who Made a Revolution A Biographical History* (Harmondsworth, 1964). A very good biography.

[202] Eugene Zaleski, *Stalinist Planning for Economic Growth* (London, 1980).

Select Bibliography – Second Edition

[203] Edwin Thomas Bacon, *The Gulag at War. Stalin's Forced Labour System in the Light of Archives* (Basingstoke, 1994). Study of OGPU camps, mainly during the war.

[204] J.D. Barber and M. Harrison, *The Soviet Home Front 1941–1945: A Social and Economic History of the USSR in World War II* (London, 1991).

[205] Francesco Benvenuti, 'Industry and Purge in the Donbass, 1936–37', *Europe-Asia Studies*, 45, 1 (1993). Study of purge at the local level.

[206] Giuseppe Boffa, *The Stalin Phenomenon* (Ithaca, 1992). English translation of 1982 survey of schools of interpretation of Stalinism.

[207] Robert Conquest, *Stalin. Breaker of Nations* (London, 1993) A portrait of Stalin.

[208] Michael David-Fox, 'Memory, Archives, Politics: The Rise of Stalin in Avtorkhanov's Technology of Power', *Slavic Review*, 54, 4 (1995). Critique of the nature and accuracy of Avtorkhanov's work.

[209] R. W. Davies, 'Economic Aspects of Stalinism', in Alec Nove (ed.), *The Stalin Phenomenon* (London, 1993). Wide-ranging discussion of the nature of the economic system.

[210] R. W. Davies, *The Industrialisation of Soviet Russia. 2. The Soviet Collective Farm 1929–1930* (London, 1980). Successor volume to [41].

[211] R. W. Davies, *The Industrialisation of Soviet Russia. 3. The Soviet Economy in Turmoil 1929–1930* (London, 1989). Successor volume to [210].

[212] R. W. Davies, 'Soviet History in the Gorbachev Revolution. The First Phase', *The Socialist Register 1988* (London, 1988).

[213] R. W. Davies, *Soviet History in the Gorbachev Revolution* (Bloomington, 1989). Discussion of Soviet revelations in the late 1980s.

[214] R. W. Davies, M. B. Tauger and S. G. Wheatcroft, 'Stalin, Grain Stocks, and the Famine of 1932–1933', *Slavic Review*, 54, 3 (1995). Argues Stalin did not have large grain stocks on hand at the time of the famine; based on archival research. Compare with [34].

[215] Charles H. Fairbanks and Susan A. Thornton, 'Soviet Decision-Making and Bureaucratic Representation: Evidence from the Smolensk Archive and an American Comparison', *Soviet Studies*, 42, 2 (1990). Study of low-level decision-making in the 1930s, based on Smolensk Archives.

[216] Sheila Fitzpatrick, 'Constructing Stalinism: Changing Western and Soviet Perspectives', in Alec Nove (ed.), *The Stalin Phenomenon* (London, 1993) Survey of different views and how they have changed.

[217] J. Arch Getty, 'The Politics of Stalinism', in Alec Nove (ed.), *The Stalin Phenomenon* (London, 1993). Survey of historiographical questions.

[218] J. Arch Getty and Roberta T. Manning (eds), *Stalinist Terror. New Perspectives* (Cambridge, 1993). Stimulating essays focusing on how the terror functioned.

[219] Mikhail Gorbachev, *October and Perestroika: the Revolution Continues* (Moscow, 1987). Report on the seventieth anniversary of the revolution.

[220] Yoran Gorlizki, 'Party Revivalism and the Death of Stalin', *Slavic Review*, 54, 1 (1995). On pressures to revive the party at the end of the Stalin period.

[221] Hans Gunther (ed.), *The Culture of the Stalin Period* (London, 1990). Papers on different aspects of culture under Stalin.

[222] James Hughes, 'Capturing the Russian Peasantry: Stalinist Grain Procurement Policy and the "Ural-Siberian Method"', *Slavic Review*, 53, 1 (1994). Study of procurement policy leading in to collectivisation.

[223] James Hughes, 'Patrimonialism and the Stalinist System: The Case of S. I. Syrtsov', *Europe–Asia Studies*, 48, 4 (1996). Syrtsov as Stalinist client.

[224] James Hughes, *Stalin, Siberia and the Crisis of the New Economic Policy* (Cambridge, 1991).

[225] Takayashi Ito (ed.), *Facing Up to the Past: Soviet Historiography Under Perestroika* (Sapporo, 1989).

[226] Amy Knight, *Beria: Stalin's First Lieutenant* (New York, 1993). Biography of Beria.

[227] Amy Knight, 'Beria and the Cult of Stalin: Rewriting Transcaucasian Party History', *Soviet Studies*, 43, 4 (1991). Beria's role in the development of the cult.

[228] Steven Kotkin, *Magnetic Mountain: Stalinism as a Civilization* (Berkeley, 1995).

[229] Nick Lampert and Gabor Rittersporn (eds), *Stalinism: Its Nature and Aftermath. Essays in Honor of Moshe Lewin* (Armonk, 1992). Essays from social history perspective.

[230] Walter Laqueur, *Stalin. The Glasnost Revelations* (London, 1990). Discussion of various aspects of the Stalin period in the light of Soviet media revelations 1987–89.

[231] Lars T. Lih, Oleg V. Naumov and Oleg V. Khlevniuk (eds), *Stalin's Letters to Molotov, 1925–1936* (New Haven, 1995). A selection of letters translated by Cathy Fitzpatrick.

[232] Steven J. Main, 'Stalin in June 1941: A Comment on Cynthia Roberts', *Europe–Asia Studies*, 48, 5 (1996). Using Stalin's appointment book, shows Stalin was very busy in the first week of the war.

[233] Rosalind Marsh, *Images of Dictatorship: Portraits of Stalin in Literature* (London, 1989).

[234] David R. Marples, 'Kuropaty: The Investigation of a Stalinist Historical Controversy', *Slavic Review*, 53, 2 (1994). Study of the mass killings at Kuropaty and responsibility for them.

[235] Elaine McClarnand, 'The Debate Continues: Views on Stalinism from the Former Soviet Union', *The Soviet and Post-Soviet Review*, 20, 1 (1993). Based on interviews with scholars in 1992.

[236] Catherine Merridale, *Moscow Politics and The Rise of Stalin. The Communist Party in the Capital, 1925–32* (New York, 1990).

[237] Frank J. Miller, *Folklore for Stalin: Russian Folklore and Pseudofolklore of the Stalin Era* (Armonk, 1990).

[238] *Molotov Remembers: Inside Kremlin Politics* (Chicago, 1993). Edited (by A. Resis) text of conversations with Molotov between 1969 and 1986.

[239] W. Moskoff, *The Bread of Affliction. The Food Supply in the USSR During World War II* (Cambridge, 1990) On the politics of food, and popular suffering.

[240] Alec Nove, *Glasnost in Action* (Boston, 1989). Discussion of revelations of glasnost.

[241] Alec Nove, 'Stalin and Stalinism – Some Introductory Thoughts', in Alec Nove (ed.), *The Stalin Phenomenon* (London, 1993). Discusses arguments about the origins, rationale, essence and nature of the Stalinist regime.

[242] Alec Nove (ed.), *The Stalin Phenomenon* (London, 1993). Collection of stimulating essays.

[243] P. Pomper, *Lenin, Trotsky and Stalin. The Intelligentsia and Power* (New York, 1990).

[244] A. D. Rassweiler, *The Generation of Power: The History of Dneprostroi*

(Oxford, 1988). Examines a major construction project of the First
Five Year Plan.

[245] E. A. Rees, *Stalinism and Soviet Rail Transport, 1928–41* (London, 1995). Operation and role of the Commissariat of the Means of Communication.

[246] Henry Reichman, 'Reconsidering "Stalinism"', *Theory and Society*, 17, 1 (1988). Study of a number of approaches.

[247] Gabor Tamas Rittersporn, 'Rethinking Stalinism', *Russian History/ Histoire Russe*, 11, 4 (1984). Discusses the diverse forces and influences at work in the 1930s.

[248] Gabor Tamas Rittersporn, *Stalinist Simplifications and Soviet Complications: Social Tensions and Political Conflicts in the USSR, 1933– 1953* (Chur, 1991). Revisionist study of the terror, translated from the French.

[249] Cynthia A. Roberts, 'Planning for the War: The Red Army and the Catastrophe of 1941', *Europe–Asia Studies*, 47, 8 (1995). Explores the dissonance between the official policy of non-provocation and the offensive deployment of Soviet troops in June 1941.

[250] Geoffrey Roberts, 'The Soviet Decision for a Pact with Nazi Germany', *Soviet Studies*, 44, 1 (1992).

[251] William G. Rosenberg and Lewis H. Siegelbaum (eds), *Social Dimensions of Soviet Industrialisation* (Bloomington, 1993). Studies of various aspects of social ramifications of industrialisation.

[252] John L. Scherer and Michael Jakobson, 'The Collectivisation of Agriculture and the Soviet Prison Camp System', *Europe–Asia Studies*, 45, 3 (1993). Study of the impact of collectivisation on the camp system.

[253] Thomas Sherlock, 'Politics and History Under Gorbachev', *Problems of Communism*, XXXVII, 3–4 (1988).

[254] Nobuo Shimotomai, *Moscow Under Stalinist Rule, 1931–34* (New York, 1991). Focus on city-level developments.

[255] Boris A. Starkov, 'The Trial that Was Not Held', *Europe–Asia Studies*, 46, 8 (1994). Study of proposed but never held Comintern trial of 1938.

[256] Robert W. Thurston, 'The Soviet Family During the Great Terror, 1935–1941', *Soviet Studies*, 43, 3 (1991). Study of the family during the purge years.

[257] Robert C. Tucker, *Stalin in Power: The Revolution from Above 1928– 1941* (New York, 1990). Continuation of [190].

[258] Arkady Vaksberg, *The Prosecutor and the Prey. Vyshinsky and the 1930s Moscow Show Trials* (London, 1990).

[259] Dmitri Volkogonov, *Stalin. Triumph and Tragedy* (London, 1991). Based on access to restricted documents and files, a significant and reliable study, but with important gaps.

[260] Chris Ward, *Stalin's Russia* (London, 1993). Text surveying developments and interpretations.

[261] Robert Weinberg, 'Purge and Politics in the Periphery: Birobidzhan in 1937', *Slavic Review*, 52, 1 (1993). Study of terror in a region;

91

based on archival sources, it shows the importance of local considerations in the purges.

[262] Stephen Welch, 'Culture, Ideology and Personality: Robert C. Tucker's Analysis of Stalinism and Soviet Politics', *Journal of Communist Studies and Transition Politics*, 12, 1 (1996). Methodological analysis of Tucker's work.

[263] Stephen Wheatcroft, 'Steadying the Energy of History and Probing the Limits of Glasnost: Moscow July to December 1987', *Australian Slavonic and East European Studies*, 1, 2 (1987). Historical revelations under glasnost.

[264] Stephen Wheatcroft, 'Unleashing the Energy of History; Mentioning the Unmentionable and Reconstructing Soviet Historical Awareness: Moscow 1987', *Australian Slavonic and East European Studies*, 1, 1 (1987). Precursor of [263].

[265] Ellen Wimberg, 'Socialism, Democratism and Criticism: The Soviet Press and the National Discussion of the 1936 Draft Constitution', *Soviet Studies*, 44, 2 (1992).

Index